CAPE
NOT REQUIRED

**You don't need to be a superhero
to find power in your life.**

**by
Cory Shepherd**

ACKNOWLEDGMENTS

My wife Danielle: I didn't learn what it meant to work hard until I realized I wanted to do whatever needs to be done to craft a life with you.

Mom & Dad: Whether by intention, commission, or omission, you made me who I am and I think I turned out pretty good.

Betsy Shepherd: You are the only one who saw the very first outline for this project, and I am so glad the final version looks nothing like the first.

Todd Rendleman: For letting me preview the path from writing to publishing.

Steve D'Annunzio: For helping me see deeper into myself than ever before.

Ron Alford: You showed me that magical place where belief meets action.

Paul Adams: A mind once stretched never
returns to its former dimensions.
Thank you for stretching me.

Vaughn Donahue: Owner of Destination Graphic,
amazing designer, and one of my oldest friends.
Thank you for bringing vision to these words.

Karen Taylor Quinn: The kindness of your insight is
matched only by its depth.

Mark Pearson: For invaluable marketing advice for
a first-time publisher.

To all my friends, family, and those who are both
at the same time—you know who you are, and I
appreciate you being there along this journey.

TABLE OF CONTENTS

FORWARD

By Steve D'Annunzio

Don't listen to me. I am certainly not objective when it comes to Cory Shepherd and his work. I'm a fan. But hear me out as to why I'm a fan, and then read this book. Not for me, or for him...but for yourself.

I own two coaching companies; one exclusively for financial planners, and the other for people who just want a better life. Having coached thousands of people over the last twenty-five years, I know something about life success and what it takes for people to achieve goals. I met Cory in this context, moments after speaking to an audience of five thousand owners and managers of the most successful financial services firms in the world. Despite being a twentysomething financial advisor among a group of graybeards, his success had earned him the right to attend this function. I did a breakout session afterwards, and Cory's participation and thoughtful questions made me sit up and take notice.

Afterward, he asked to work with me personally, going on to invest more money in learning and life success than most advisors do in a lifetime. He was like a dry sponge around water, soaking up the best we had to offer. When given an assignment, he completed every time, on time. His efforts propelled new results; he hit his goals and then went beyond. He went from making not only a big living, to making a big difference in the lives of his clients. Cory is a mission-driven man, and that makes him truly unique.

While some clients I work with are negative and difficult to coach, every time I saw Cory's name on my calendar, my spirit would light up. He was a joy to teach and to be around. He was the kind of student that made me optimistic about the future. After a few years, a shift began to occur. He continued to positively receive the coaching, but also began explaining it differently, using his own words, stories and principles. He was developing his own unique message, one that I sensed needed to be heard by others. He was transforming from successful student into functional teacher.

In his book *The Art of Power*, Pulitzer-prize winner John Meacham chronicles the life of Thomas Jefferson. We glimpse the successes and struggles of this powerful man, but alas, are not given insight into the success skills that made him so. In *Cape Not Required*, it is precisely those kinds of skills that Cory reveals in detail. Though these skills are extraordinary, they are explained in an ordinary but fun way, making them understandable and applicable for us all. Cory has a gift for taking very complex concepts and explaining them simply. While many success books preach to you, this one speaks to you as a friend and an equal.

To my knowledge there are few worthy books written about power, what it is, how to develop it, and most importantly how to use it for good. One of them is *Power vs. Force*, in which author David Hawkins puts power into context for all good people to understand. "Power" is energy used with a positive purpose, fueling any goal that uplifts and helps humanity. Conversely, "force" is energy used for an oppressive purpose, fueling goals that diminish and hurt humanity. Energy is neutral; but its intention distinguishes power from force. This book's intention is clear: to alleviate the suffering inherent to the human condition and improve the welfare of all people.

Why is it critically important for you to know this? To do good in the world, to accomplish your own life goals, to be happier, healthier, and wealthier, you need power. You need to learn what it is, what drains it out of you, and how to conserve and compound it. It is one of the great truths of life success. But as guitarist Jimi Hendrix famously said, "when the power of love overcomes the love of power, the world will know peace." Real "power" is derived from the power of love, while "force" is a consequence of the love of power. Jimi was a Seattle native, like my friend and colleague Cory Shepherd, who has written a gift of love for us with this book. You don't have to be a hero to read and use it—just someone who cares about living a good life. Please read it out of self-love. I know that if you apply its ideas, your life will be far better.

Steve D'Annunzio

Rochester NY
November 2016

WHAT IS POWER AND IS IT OKAY TO WANT IT?

Many people think of power in a negative context. The power-hungry politician or executive certainly contribute to that context, and we've come to think of power as a corrupting force; an unstoppable pursuit of self-interest while crushing others. While I agree that some people use power that way, I have come to understand it differently. My context for power is as a neutral energy; a capacity to accomplish a result. Take horsepower in an automobile, for example—its power can enhance our lives, letting us roam larger distances; or, it can just as easily be misused, as in reckless accidents. In either case, the charge of positive or negative flows from the wielder, not from the power itself.

I wrote this book around the belief that we can build power while continuously doing good, and for the purpose of bringing greater value into the world. Furthermore, it is the responsibility of those with noble goals and love in their hearts to each fulfill their unique capacity for growing and using power, lest we leave the world solely in the hands of those whose hearts are hungry for power only for power's sake. For the purpose of our work together here, power is about directing and coordinating your creative energy effectively, to generate more positive value in the world. The concepts in this book all come back to practicing ways of communicating, moving, and being that add value to the lives of those around us—adding value to our *own* lives at the same time.

All my life I have been fascinated by the way the world works, and what happens underneath the surface or behind the scenes. I got into science fiction in my youth, because there was always a possibility of truth in the stories. Because the fiction had a root in science, I hoped that if we were only able to complete our understanding of the world, the story really could be true. Then I started to discover that much of today's most cutting-edge science is in fact so miraculous that it could read like a science fiction novel to those of us discovering it for the first time. So if anything I bring up sounds too cosmic or "science fictional," I completely understand. I don't expect you to buy it all at first; I simply encourage you to try it on like a new jacket, to see how it fits before you buy.

Through studying our physical world, physicists discovered and mapped out several laws that describe constant properties of the universe in which we live. One of those laws, called "Conservation of Energy and Matter," says that energy and matter cannot be created or destroyed, only transformed into various forms. We see evidence of this when water moves from ice to liquid to steam—the form may change, but the total amount of substance stays constant.

Since energy can't be created or destroyed, what we call "creativity" is not the act of creating new energy, but tapping into the already existing energy in our universe, and using it to create new possibility in our lives. The more possibility you create for a greater number of people, the greater the amount of value you will add to the world.

I'm a financial advisor by trade, so you might assume that when I talk about value, I'm talking about money. I will address some thoughts on money along the way, but this is not a financial book. Although no one attempting to build and maintain large stores of money will be able to do so without developing power, power as a resource is much greater than money. That's because money is two-dimensional, while power is all around, in 3D. There are many things money cannot buy, but power is an energy and currency that can create anything we hope for in life.

Think of a personal hero, whether an athlete, musician, humanitarian, philanthropist, politician, or mogul. Whomever you revere, he or she only came to make an impact by gathering and directing power. If you are out to make a similar kind of positive impact in the world, becoming more powerful is the only way to begin your noble quest.

How Do We Get Power?

Superheroes in popular culture, from the actual superhuman, like Spider-Man and Superman, to the highly driven and well-equipped, like Batman, all have powers that seem miraculous when compared to we mere humans. Super powers come from mystic, scientific, alien, or accidental sources, and we can easily transfer our beliefs about those heroes and how they acquire power to real-life humans whose powers *seem* superhuman. Professional athletes, entrepreneurs and titans of industry, classmates voted most likely to succeed—we come to wonder about the advantages that gave them the power to accomplish such feats of strength and renown.

For some, luck and circumstance can help—or hurt. On a worldwide spectrum of headstarts, I know I benefited from the instant advantage and security provided by the mix of geography, nationality, gender, and economic stability I was born into. I *also* know that I lack certain physical advantages around height and muscle composition that mean I'll just never be a professional athlete. In other words, context matters. None of us has unlimited power in every domain.

Physical power is often more limited than mental, although our physical power is often greater than we believe. For example, I ran competitive long distance in high school. Because I received amazing coaching as part of a community of runners, I accrued greater power in running than any other athletic activity in my life. As a result of belief that grew from that power, I continually set new personal records and graduated as a member of a three-time State Championship cross country team, even though my body, often described as "husky" at the time, was not "built like a runner's." As we'll see, power and belief are closely intertwined.

If you wanted to start a painting company, for example, you wouldn't actually need to know anything about owning companies or painting. You would only need to become powerful in sharing your dream in a way that convinces other people with the necessary skills to go there with you. Mark Zuckerberg did not alone possess all the skills necessary to make Facebook into what it is today. He *did*, however, have just the right combination of skills to light a spark, and to enroll the right people in pursuing his dream. He led his team at a genius level, attracting other people who added their own power to his vision, and that made all the difference.

We are all capable of heroic feats, and we all have access to motivational evidence from people like Mark Zuckerberg, so why don't we all achieve Facebook-like success on a regular basis? Because there is safety in stasis. And challenging that stasis will be your first step toward building greater power.

CHAPTER 1

BUILDING YOUR INNER POWER

- ➢ Meet Your Ego
- ➢ Meditation For the Rest of Us
- ➢ Affirmation Statements
- ➢ True vs. Useful
- ➢ Valid vs. Powerful

Meet Your Ego

Have you ever thought these kinds of thoughts?

I am not good enough.

Who am I to accomplish that?

If someone else hasn't already done that, it must not be possible.

Why would they want me?

Where do those kinds of questions and comments come from? They come from the mind inside of our minds, which I call the Ego. Most of us hear "ego" and we think of the stuck-up person who thinks very highly of himself. That is one part, but not the whole, of this force inside of us. (The modern understanding of "Ego" came from Sigmund Freud, and I will continue to use Ego in reference to that idea, though I will likely take the conversation places Freud never intended.)

Our Ego is a self-preservation mechanism that our early human ancestors experienced in a more basic form, and has grown along with us in intelligence over the millennia. Yes, our Ego is the part of every one of us that enables us to think very highly of ourselves and appear arrogant to others. But the Ego isn't focused on looking better than others. What the Ego really clings to is the current condition or state of our development—your Ego seeks to maintain you exactly as you are *right now*. To the Ego, change is dangerous, staying the same is safe, and the Ego's only job is to flee danger for safety.

The Ego had a much simpler job early in the history of *Homo sapiens*. "Hunt and avoided being hunted" was life's basic condition, so we simply had to master a few basics of pattern recognition. Changes to our environment like the movement of a shadow, a swish in the grass, or the crack of a stick, were all likely to mean a predator was stalking nearby, triggering evasive maneuvers from the early Ego.

Today, a change to our environment like a new project, a promotion, or a public speaking obligation is not likely to come with actual physical consequences no matter how poorly we perform, yet our Ego only has one response—the same response to a perceived life-and-death threat. Change of any kind, even in a logically beneficial direction, is still a step into the unknown, and the Ego regards that step as a leap out of an aircraft without a parachute.

To reboot our minds and promote positive change, we can either help our Ego develop more powerful interpretations of the world around us, or create strategies for giving our Ego the afternoon off. Either approach begins a lifelong journey, because our Ego is slippery and adaptable. The moment we reach a goal, or find a new position in life, our Ego becomes attached to that new frame of existence, and every time we change, we need to start the cycle again. Wherever you are in that cycle, you are never too early or too late to jump in. Training your Ego is a process of self-discovery, and the first step is to notice your current state of mind.

Meditation for the Rest of Us

The concept of meditation often comes with religious, or even mystic, connotations. This might make you uncomfortable if you don't consider yourself a spiritual person, don't have a context for meditation in your religious background, or are just a type-A American who has trouble sitting still not *doing* anything for more than five minutes. I use meditation as a practical tool to collect my thoughts, calm my busy brain, and connect to the most important ideas in my head on any given day.

Many high-level athletes and business people use meditation as a key performance driver. In fact, many people credit meditation with a wide range of benefits, from the physiologic (reducing blood pressure) to the mystic (encountering divine presence). Early on in my meditation practice, I chose to focus on as grounded and practical an application as possible: helping my brain become a more hospitable home for my thoughts.

I am that typical type-A person. Like sharks evolved to constantly move through the water, I felt like I always needed to move toward a goal, and at first meditation seemed closer to hibernation. I had to "trick" myself into meditating at first, and now I look forward to my 15–30 minutes every morning. In fact, if I skip meditating for too many days in a row, I start to feel a little foggy in the head. That's because meditation clears a path to real, "normal" brain function, so when I meditate less, it's easy to notice the gradual relapse to a cluttered, muddled state of mind.

One important warning: Meditation is first and foremost a chance to listen to what goes on in our heads. This means that if you're uneasy with yourself and your thoughts, meditation could be uncomfortable. Especially if you're working through a mental health condition, consult your doctor to make sure meditation makes sense for you.

Here is how I recommend trying meditation for the first time, to get past any skepticism from your Ego:

Step 1: Set a timer on your phone for one minute.

Step 2: Sit so you're comfortable.

Step 3: Close your eyes, and sit there until your alarm sounds, with no goal other than to see what happens.

Ready... Go!

Did you self-destruct? Did someone come yell at you for meditating? My guess is no. As your thoughts acclimate to the concept of time alone with themselves, you can extend the timer on your phone to 10, 15, or 30 minutes. There are prolific meditators who go for much longer than that, but I encourage you to keep your commitment minimal at least until you've made meditation a habit.

Meditating for 15–30 minutes 5–6 times a week has much greater benefits than meditating for an hour once a week and then giving up after two weeks because the rest of your schedule gets in the way.

You can also integrate contemplative music or a guided meditation recording if you find that helpful. A quick internet search for "meditation apps" will give you lots of options. I currently use an app called Brain.fm, and I've also heard great things about Headspace, Calm, and Holosync.

What you will probably experience as you extend your meditation time is a lively stream of thought bubbles popping off left and right:

> *I can't believe I am meditating...... What is that smell? Smells like popcorn....like at the movies....I really love Star Wars...Empire is the best....What was the name of that creature that Luke had to wrap himself inside to survive the night on Hoth?....H-O-T-H, Hoth....Why does a snow planet have a name that contains the word "hot" inside it? ....Hot Pockets, yum.*

Meditating will show you what a loud place your mind can be. The act of internal listening is very powerful, because by merely listening, we create a fundamental shift of perspective—a separation between ourselves and that stream of consciousness. The Ego changes from "me" to "something in my head." By creating a separation between "me" and "my thoughts," that stream of consciousness goes from *being you*, to something that is merely *happening* to you. Long before we decide whether or not to listen to the Ego, it creates the reality we live in; the thoughts from our Ego happen deep inside us—so deep that we can't detect any separation between them and us.

Once you become practiced at observing the Ego's thoughts, you can create two diverging points of view: yours, and your Ego's—the latter to which you can subscribe or unsubscribe at will. Meditation can also help create a separation between you and the reactionary feelings your brain creates as automatic chemical responses to events in the world around you. Like a time-delay broadcast of live television, you can develop the ability to see reactionary emotions coming, choose how you will respond to them, and curate what you broadcast to the world.

Once you're more comfortable hearing your own thoughts as they occur, you can start to reprogram your deepest code. By choosing particular thoughts to dwell on, either while you are meditating or at strategic moments throughout the day, you can teach your Ego new default responses.

Affirmation Statements

Personal affirmation statements turn the tide of the negative self-talk our Ego inflicts upon us every day. The constant stream of status quo maintenance-statements that come from deep in our minds reinforce a central message: "You are exactly where you are because that is where you belong." You are only still reading this if deep down you want more out of life than what you currently experience, so that message only works for the Ego, not any other part of us. But the Ego is loud and powerful; it is even talking to me right now, telling me "no one would want to read what you write," and "nothing you can say here will help anyone."

That dissenting voice was almost enough to keep me from sitting down to write this morning, but I was armed with a list of affirmation statements that I had prepared in advance, for such a time as this. I need to thank my friend Ron Alford, an amazing coach and partner with Southwestern Consulting, for helping me develop this discipline.

The idea is to accept that negative thoughts will creep into our minds regularly, and that those thoughts will have the potential to negatively impact our actions. Just like the Federal Emergency Management Agency (FEMA) developing and drilling emergency response scenarios before they happen, we can develop a plan to combat "negative creep" before it occurs. It is almost impossible to say something out loud and think a different thought in our head at the same time, so this list of affirmation statements are meant to be spoken aloud. I find it helpful to say a few phrases out loud before meditation, then keep one of the phrases in my thoughts as I meditate.

I designed affirmation statements to help me with my writing, specifically to combat all the negative self-talk my Ego creates. Here is what I said this morning to help fire up my brain and ignite my energy to write:

"My book is the answer to someone's prayer."

"The kind of conviction that attracts many also repels a few."

"I am a bestselling author and I have a life-changing message to share with the world."

I intentionally crafted each of these statements to neutralize a specific element of the resistance my own Ego manifests, and you can employ the same technique with your unique areas of resistance. As you start to plan a new and challenging path toward a goal, pay attention to the fear that pops up as you think about moving into action. As you identify the thoughts behind the fear, write down a sentence that expresses how you would like to feel in the absence of that fear.

Here are the whys behind the three statements I shared:

My first fear was that I would spend huge amounts of energy writing a book, and it would create zero additional value in the world. *"My book is the answer to someone's prayer"* reminds me that there are so many people out there in the world, and that just by pure chance, there has to be at least one person for whom my words matter. Whatever new venture or goal you face, there is guaranteed to be at least one person out there whose life would be similarly changed if you can accomplish your work.

Second, I like to get along with people in general, and I worried that I would create anti-fans by speaking clearly about deep topics in a public forum. *"The kind of conviction that attracts many also repels a few"* reminds me that the kind of passion that inspires at least one person is equally likely to repel other people, and that is just fine. It's best to measure success in these matters like a baseball batting average: it's the number of successes that matters, not the number of failures. Furthermore, hitting successfully only three times out of ten is enough to propel athletes to the Hall of Fame.

Finally, the third statement: *I am a bestselling author and I have a life-changing message to share with the world.* This one is more about promoting general confidence than confronting a fear. I wrote it because it makes me smile at its sheer audacity. Maybe by the time you read this, I will be a bestselling author. If so, I would love if you sent me a tweet @coryshepherd to say "Congratulations, you made it!" On the morning that I write this, I have not yet received a congratulatory call from Amazon or the *New York Times*. I haven't even published the book yet! Do they even make a congratulatory call to an author when he gets on that list? I don't know!

What I do know is that to create *any* kind of amazing change in our lives, we must suspend disbelief, and act as if we truly *remember* a future we have not yet seen. By repeating affirming phrases over and over, your brain starts believing the ideas could be true, and your whole way of being starts a subtle transformation. Hundreds of little reactions and responses shift over time, and as you start acting more and more as if your goal has come true, you actually pull yourself closer and closer to realizing that goal. Remember, belief and power are so closely intertwined that it is often impossible to know where one stops and the other starts.

Now that we can identify the Ego and better control all the thoughts swarming around in our heads, we can move deeper into two distinctions around how we use our thoughts, and how we interact with the thoughts and ideas that other people have. The first distinction, *True versus Useful*, helps us curate our internal response to the world around us. The second, *Valid versus Powerful*, helps us curate our external response to the opinions of others.

True vs. Useful

Now that you can recognize the kind of perspectives the Ego throws at you constantly, you can go one step beyond accepting or declining those perspectives, by inserting new ones of your own. The idea is that you could purposefully choose some viewpoints that may or may not be true, may be impossible to prove true, or may very likely not be true, but could be very useful. I first encountered this concept while reading *The Charisma Myth* by Olivia Fox Cabane. One passage in particular played out in my life the very morning I read it.

I was driving into my office, and before I even got out of my neighborhood, on a very quiet street with no other cars in sight, a woman in a sedan backed out of her driveway right in front of me. She could have easily waited two or three seconds, and neither of us would have been inconvenienced, but as it happened I was forced to slam on my brakes, throwing my body forward, jarring me out of my morning calm. I felt a flush over my face, and a few choice words came to mind. Normally I would have stewed throughout the drive, and upon arriving at work, told the first three people I saw my tale of righteous indignation, carrying the emotion of that interaction through the rest of my day.

But on that day, in that moment, I interrupted my normal reactive pattern. I remembered the concept of *cognitive reappraisal* that Cabane discussed, which I adapted to think of as *True vs. Useful*. What if I could replace the default story of anger with a different story, one that would create a more positive emotional context for me at the start to my day. Since we can often only guess at the motivation for others' actions, why not invent a motivation that promotes a positive response. Here is what I invented:

This woman's name is Jen. She has one sister, Tina, the only family she has left in the world. Tina is pregnant and the baby daddy is completely out of the picture. Jen just got the following text from Tina:

Water just broke!
The baby is coming!

Jen leaps into her car to speed off to her sister's aid. As she leaves her driveway, Jen sees me coming out of the corner of her eye. In that split second, she knows she can complete her maneuver without causing an accident and speeds away, whispering apologies under her breath as she goes. She gets there in time for her sister's labor. After her nephew is born, Tina tells her, "I am so glad you made it, I could not have done this without you."

I started to root for "Jen" in the midst of a story I had made up, and suddenly I wasn't angry anymore. I created a context that was not necessarily *true*, but was much more *useful*. My creative liberty did nothing to mislead or hurt anyone else, and saved me from a morning full of distraction and negativity. I am not suggesting that there is no objective or moral truth. Just simply that most of the meaning we ascribe to events in our everyday lives is meaning we made up anyway, so why not edit the internal monologue to produce more powerful and positive outcomes?

Valid vs. Powerful

True versus Useful is a principal primarily intended for internal, personal use. Its cousin, *Valid versus Powerful* is about connecting with others. Many of us believe our opinions to be "TRUTH." The best example of this is every election cycle in recent history, where millions of people on social media appear to treat their political opinions as gospel, and everyone who disagrees as a buffoon. From Bush to Clinton to Obama to Trump, it happens every time. Most political conversation quickly falls into chaos because it involves two people who believe they know the TRUTH, trying to prove each other wrong.

No one *purposely* believes something illogical; they simply cling to the most logical thought that could possibly come from the sum total of all the information they have received in their lives. This means we cannot automatically assume someone is an idiot for thinking what they think, simply because their thoughts differ from ours. Instead, we need to accept that everyone's beliefs are valid in the context in which they were created.

Early in my career I came across clients who practiced some incredibly stupid financial habits—at least that is what I thought at the time. I never told them I thought they were stupid, at least not in those words. But since then, I've taken this phrase to heart—I've come to call it the Principle of Consistency:

"How you are anywhere is how you are everywhere."

If I was thinking internally, "what a dummy, this person is doing it all wrong," then I was certainly communicating that message to my clients in all kinds of subtle ways. Maybe so subtle that neither of us would consciously realize it, but definitely communicating negativity to the point where that couple did not remain my clients over the long term.

I invite you to join me in cultivating the assumption that everyone acts as prudently as possible with the information and resources available to them. Fair warning, living this philosophy is hard! Let's look at an extreme example: Someone who uses shopping as therapy for whatever he is unhappy about, using a credit card to enable those purchases, and accruing crippling debt along the way. In the past I would have thought, "clearly that is in no way the right thing to do; we have to fix this." But now, I just don't believe anyone needs to be fixed. Everyone has elements in their lives that others would call flaws, even those we regard as heroes. (*Especially* those we regard as heroes!) We are all perfectly imperfect, doing the most we can with what we have.

I had never realized how many times a day I subtly made others wrong to feel more validation in my own beliefs, until I took a break from doing so. Now, instead of pushing other people down, or secretly judging them for being wrong, I have the opportunity to *help them discover a more powerful interpretation.* So that person accruing crippling debt through "retail therapy" isn't wrong and doesn't need to be fixed; he is only doing what he is doing because he has not yet discovered a more powerful path.

> *ALL interpretations = valid*
> *ALL interpretations ≠ powerful*

An immediate consequence of this philosophy is that you will achieve fewer moments of righteous satisfaction. If you revel in any opportunity to prove someone wrong, to win an argument, or otherwise demonstrate your unimpeachable greatness, you will need to find other sources of joy. Instead of proving people wrong, or even proving yourself right, try seeking greater power.

Remember, if they are not wrong, that means you are not right. Neither of you hold the "TRUTH." If you believe (and can illustrate with evidence) that you have a more powerful interpretation, then your duty is to honor the other person's belief, and help him discover the greater power available in the interpretation to which you subscribe.

The amazing outcome of living this philosophy is that you stop making enemies, and start collecting allies. The person that you "prove wrong" around the water cooler in front of several other colleagues will never be your ally, and he may retreat further into his less powerful opinion just out of a desire to preserve his dignity. The person whom you validate, then help discover greater power in another point of view—*that* person becomes your raving fan forever.

CHAPTER 2

WANDERING IN A STRAIGHT LINE

> ➤ Defining Success
> ➤ Avoid Competition
> ➤ Layers of Knowledge
> ➤ Pad Your Personal Lottery

Defining Success

Success is a tricky concept. Lots of people would say they know what it looks like, without actually being able to define it. They might define success as something like having a lot of money, but with the quick caveat, "that's not all it is." Success can only be defined in context, and context is usually missing in conversations around success.

LeBron James is a successful basketball player by all accounts, yet what if his life's goal had been to grow the best vegetables known to humankind on the farm that he started as a legacy for future generations? If basketball came out of some other compulsive drive for fame that he couldn't control, I might not consider him so successful in the context of his dream.

What truly makes us feel happy and successful is a very personal and unique equation for each of us. I know some amazing people who won't make much money in life and don't have a high-powered career, but who passionately invest themselves in a pursuit they love, routinely changing the lives of people around them.

People often think that success requires time away from other important areas of life, like family. I think this *can* be true; I also think that statements like "I don't want to take too much time away from my family" can become self-limiting when used as a disclaimer for why a dream can't come true. The

more powerful question to ask is: "How could I do
_____, while also supporting an amazing re-
lationship with my family?" Still, you may need time
to dive head-first into something new, and I invite
you to ask this followup question: "Would my family/
friends/children rather trade some amount of time in
the near future to have the fullest version of me, or
would they rather give up no time at all, and have a
regretful version of me for the rest of my life?"

This chapter is about building a strong foun-
dation at the beginning of the long road you will
travel.

Avoid Competition

*"If you knew how long and hard I worked for
my art, you wouldn't find it as wonderful."*
—Michelangelo

The media glamorizes certain kinds of success—
business, art, and entertainment mostly. What is
nigh unmentioned is the blood, sweat, and tears
that go into fulfilling big dreams. Most puff piec-
es on gold-medal athletes lend lip service to the
hard work they put in, and spend the lion's share
of airtime reliving victorious moments second by
second. Most people operating at the top of their
fields spent years getting there. Anyone who looks
like they popped onto the scene with instant success probably built transferrable skills in another

discipline, and all we got to see was the fireworks at the end.

Although the long road might seem intimidating, you really wouldn't want it any other way. That long road is your competitive advantage. In occupations or pursuits where there is no barrier to entry, competition is extremely fierce, whatever you're offering becomes commoditized, and it becomes more and more difficult to reap reward for your work. Compare a Subway "sandwich artist" and Picasso, for example: Who took longer to reach the peak of their career, and who faced greater competition? I don't know the success rate and completion time of Subway University students, but I assume that Picasso's education and the refinement of his craft took far longer.

But in the question of competition, the positions are reversed. There are always more sandwich artists clamoring to fill an empty spot on the line, and while there are also many painters in the world, there is only one Picasso. Pablo created his legacy by *not* competing. He did not try to be better than everyone in the mainstream of art; he created his own space where there was no other competition. Time spent carving out a unique niche often means a greater reward.

Layers of Knowledge

In any given field there are probably infinite layers of knowledge, but for now, I want to talk about two:

the basics, and mastery. Though we certainly won't achieve mastery if we stay on the basics forever, we must master the basics before we can achieve great things. Ralph Waldo Emerson once wrote, "The man who grasps *principles* can successfully select his own *methods*. The man who tries *methods*, ignoring *principles*, is sure to have trouble." In other words, you need the basics if you're ever going to go beyond them.

Anything that is "common knowledge" is widely available information, so by definition you won't create value by simply sharing that knowledge. Continuing Education (C.E.) is required in many fields, but it is not a competitive advantage, because everyone has to do it! Any course or seminar that earns you C.E. credit for your profession only got approved for that program because it fit into the framework of your industry. Relying only on that knowledge will not lead to unique creation, it'll only lead to maintaining common practice and doing what everyone else is doing. However, *this doesn't mean you can skip the basics*. Picasso and sandwich artists alike need to start with the foundational principles of their crafts in order to achieve great things. Being too proud to be a beginner is a certain recipe for sudden failure.

I once read a rumor about Leonardo Da Vinci, that he could draw a perfect circle freehand. Whether or not that is true, let's call it *useful* for this conversation. What is very useful is to note that the artist who may be most widely known for creating the *Mona Lisa*, and who is literally the original Renaissance man, that person went to great lengths to understand the smallest building blocks of his craft. To draw a perfect circle unaided, I imagine he had to draw thousands and thousands of circles.

There's a common theme among those who achieve mastery in their crafts, and that is humility. A lesser artist would consider it below his genius to sit there drawing circle after circle. "I am being kept from from the real masterpiece I want to create," he might say. Only the Da Vincis of the world would recognize all those circles as *part* of their future masterpieces. In Da Vinci's time, canvas was expensive and paint could be easily covered over to use a surface anew, so people often speculate about what might be hidden underneath a master work like the *Mona Lisa*. We know the secret—it's all circles.

What are the circles in your field? What are the pursuits that most of your peers would say "that's a waste of time—I have bigger things to achieve!" If you are willing to go that deep and really master the basics, you will eventually achieve more than anyone around you. Except you won't notice, because you'll be too busy quietly creating a body of work that everyone *else* will notice.

Several times a year, I fly somewhere in the country to attend gatherings of the best minds in my industry and learn from people who are actively putting their knowledge to use. I receive no CE credit, and often must pay for the privilege of learning. Finding active practitioners is important, because any time I see someone has started only teaching the thing they are doing, I wonder if something's off. My favorite example is the "experts" who sell a book or a whole course (usually on infomercials at 2am) about a "proven method for getting rich quick." Whether that's a hot new home-based business or investing in pork bellies, when I see those advertisements I wonder why they would even share this amazing secret if it is so good. Is it possible that they can more safely and predictably make money by selling other people on the idea, rather than actually doing it?

Perhaps even more important than seeking active experts in your industry is to seek the best minds in disciplines *outside* your own. Find people on the cutting edge of any field, and you can probably take something about what they're doing or how they think, back to your industry. This is how you grow in giant leaps—by seeking new ways of thinking, ways that are truly unique to your area of expertise, and using those to do something no one else like you is doing! If flying across the country is not financially feasible right now, there are a host of online coaches and teaching programs that can help you get started for much less than the price of a plane ticket. Start by searching for "coach" + "your field" and you will likely get a few choices to research and compare.

If personal coaching and flying across the country just aren't workable for you right now, then there is still an incredible resource that gives free or nearly free intimate access to some of the best minds in the world, alive or dead: books! There are so many books out there; chances are good someone has written a book about how to be or do whatever you are dreaming about doing. However, people often treat reading a book like an event, when in fact, creating a relationship with that book would produce so much more. Several years ago I started keeping a monthly list of the books I read. This was partially to brag to colleagues about how many books I was reading, but primarily to help me keep track of a growing list of business mentors I could return to time and time again. It is amazing to think that I can learn from some of history's greatest thought leaders, even those long dead before my birth, for the small price of a paperback or ebook.

Padding Your Personal Lottery

Have you ever heard the cliché that success is all about being in the right place at the right time? That is often true, but false in the context that most people receive it. While coincidences happen to lots of people, high performers don't rely on coincidence. The correlation effect is what high-level players seek—being in the right place at the right time is a lot more likely to happen if you more often put yourself into situations that might be "the right place." Like every state lottery says, you can't win if you don't buy a ticket. Whatever new goal you want to make real right now, you can give yourself profoundly better odds than winning the lottery, but you have to make sure you buy your tickets.

Every action you take that results in even a tiny movement in the right general direction buys you one ticket. Every person you ask to help you is more like five entries, because now you are overlapping your personal lottery with theirs and either one of you winning is likely to help the other reach their goal. Every time you gain a piece of new knowledge that strengthens your abilities, that is an entry. Just make sure you buy yourself tickets every single day, and pretty soon correlation will lead to causation.

Do you know that person that just seems incapable of failing? The annoying person who just seems to excel at anything she touches? What you didn't see were all the little lottery tickets she bought herself over the years. By the time you start noticing her, she is harvesting the benefits of years of hard work planting seeds. It is not hard to win when every drawing comes out of a bucket filled with thousands of tickets with your name on them. Anyone you might consider an overnight success knows how long it takes to become an overnight success. They all bought themselves life raffle tickets for many years before they got the chance to pull the winning ticket.

CHAPTER 3

FROM INSPIRATION TO REALIZATION: FOUR STEPS TO HIT YOUR GOAL, AND WHY TYPICAL GOAL SETTING DOESN'T WORK

> ➢ Get Clear On What You Really Want
> ➢ Inspiration To Realization
> ➢ Write It Down
> ➢ Tell No One
> ➢ Keep Score
> ➢ Mark the End

There is a huge distinction between goal setting, and goal keeping. Dreaming dreams and setting goals is fun, exciting, and frankly, easy. We are talking about great things we are going to do, versus actually facing the emotional strain of following through. There is an art to setting goals that are high enough to be meaningful, and in-reach enough to be doable. As far as defining doable, well, the great titans of our world probably set ridiculously unreachable goals, and just kept figuring it out along the way, so don't let anyone else define for you what is reasonable or unreasonable. At the same time, don't throw a huge mountain in front of yourself just because some guru told you to dream big. If you have zero belief you could get to the top, you will never even start the climb.

Get Clear On What You Really Want

What do you want in life?

Money as a goal will only get us so far. Extensive research in recent years proves that money can help buy happiness, but only up to a certain point. $50,000–$70,000 of annual income is the point of diminished marginal return. After that, more money could certainly be a goal for its own sake, but it won't bring any additional happiness or fulfillment. Above 70k, it can't be about the money anymore.

We need some inspiring and specific reasons for what we are going to do with the additional money we are after.

Buying more stuff doesn't work. I certainly like toys myself, and having been down this road, I implore you to be cautious here. Buying an extensive collection of things requires our time to care for and use those things. It isn't that chasing possessions can't be motivating, it can. Setting a goal to buy a new Audi A8 may actually inspire you to put in the extra effort needed to pull in the income that gets you the car. It's just that I have seen a lot of people hit that kind of possession goal and then discover their newfound happiness is hollow.

In their book *Happy Money*, Elizabeth Dunn and Michael Norton talk about the correlation between cars and happiness. One of their observations hit me like a ton of bricks: When someone is stuck in traffic in their BMW or Audi, they are not thinking about how awesome it is to be in a BMW or Audi, they are thinking about how awful it is to be stuck in traffic! Since I can't hear your reaction to that news, I am going to assume you still want the Audi, and that is great. But, instead of setting the car as your goal, start by setting a goal for some kind of impact you can make in the world, and make sure it's valuable enough to other people that the activity also generates the money you need to get that dream car. That way, when you are eventually stuck in traffic in your Audi, you can also be grateful for all the impact that you have made.

While you may think a car will motivate you, according to Dunn and Norton, the scientifically most gratifying way to spend money is on experiences. Buy "stuff" and it will crumble over time. Buy the creation of a wonderful memory, and it actually grows more favorable over time! Not only does the memory improve with time, years of reliving the memory may actually bring us *more* joy than the original event. Have you ever rewatched a movie or television show you remember loving as a kid? I would urge you not to, because every time I have taken that trip down memory lane, the memory proved to be better than the actual experience. By the same principle, most amazing memories you create now will bring you even more pleasure in the future than they do today. The most gratifying experiences are those that demonstrate generosity to others, so take your mom out to lunch, take your kids or nieces and nephews to the zoo, or surprise your significant other with an activity she loves when she least expects it.

Inspiration To Realization

There are plenty of books out there that will help you set a goal and keep it. I have read many of them, and a common narrative always appears that I simply don't agree with. The narrative is: Decide on your goal, decide by when you will do it, *then do everything in your power to let every single person you know hear your goal and your timeline for achieving it*. The logic here is if everyone in your life knows what you said you were going to do, and by when, then you will have no choice but to move heaven and earth to make that goal happen, lest you suffer the shame and discredit of failing in front of everyone in your life. There are two issues with this strategy:

1. It creates a negative context around your wonderful, positive goal.

2. It assumes (incorrectly) that you have complete control over all the variables related to achieving your goal, especially those related to the timeline.

In response to discovering these two problems, I crafted a four-step process for taking a goal from inspiration to realization:

1. Write It Down

The act of creating written plans is a legal requirement to prove guilt in a conspiracy. Without writing anything down, it's difficult to make progress on anything more than the simplest tasks. In order to see complex, long-term goals come to fruition, we need to create a written body of evidence around what we set out to do. Our lawmakers knew this to be true, so they defined conspiracy to filter out the mostly harmless people who do nothing but talk, from the dangerous people willing to put nefarious thought into action. When setting a goal, pretend you are the ringleader of a conspiracy, trying to provide enough evidence to be proven guilty of conspiring toward your goal. Be slightly dangerous to your Ego and its existing condition; set yourself apart from the "mostly harmless" people who only sit around and talk about how life could be better.

Write down as much about *why* you are creating this goal as *what* the goal actually is. If you are unhappy with your current life situation, what are you most dissatisfied with, and how is making this new goal real going to alleviate that pain for you? Remember that the only courtroom here is in your mind. There is a long road ahead, and you are going to forget why you started down this path. You will be the only judge and jury, so you need this body of proof later, to find the conviction to persist through the final hurdles.

Simply put, perseverance is creating a "memory" of the future, and holding it in our minds long enough for that memory to become real. Here at the beginning of your journey, imagine how you would feel living in this new reality, and write down as much detail as possible.

2. Tell No One

While building a financial firm of 30 advisors, I saw this scene play out many times: In the midst of an amazingly empowering and energizing goal-setting pump-up session (usually a beginning-of-the-year kickoff and business planning meeting), an advisor chooses to reach higher than she has ever reached before. She sets a goal to grow her business 40% over the next year. Then, during group sharing time, she hears a colleague declare he wanted to shoot for 100% growth in his business over the next year. Our hero gets caught up in the excitement and decides in a split second that 40% is too little. "I am going for double too!" she announces.

Then she rushes home in excitement and tells her spouse all the amazing things that are going to happen over the next year. She tells her kids they are going to stay at the *nice* hotel at Disney this year; she tells her parents she is finally going to be able to pay back that long-term loan; the whole family goes out to dinner to celebrate success yet to come.

Monday rolls around, and the adrenaline-dopamine milkshake has worn off. There is actual work to do; emotionally challenging work. She has to start reaching out to a *lot* (remember this was a 100% increase) of people who all have the power to say *no* to her, and are actually more statistically likely to decline than say yes. Maybe her plans work out, but more likely life doesn't go perfectly, and at the end of week two, she is already 70% off pace. That isn't insurmountable over just two weeks, but now, doubt and fear start creeping in. Doubt that she can really do this, and fear of what her family and friends with think of her failure. All the people that she thought she was enlisting to help now un-wittingly become demons in her mind. Every per-son she told about her big goal is someone she has the opportunity to disappoint.

Instead of failing miserably and publicly, our advisor starts to build a set of rationalizations for why she can't or shouldn't do what she originally set out to do. Now not only is she most certainly not going to hit her goal this year; she may nev-er hit that higher level of business because of the mental walls she has built to protect herself from disgrace.

This is why when I set a goal...**I.DO.NOT.TELL. ANYONE!**

Which isn't actually true, I just like to capitalize on the chance to create one of those dramatic all-bold-with-a-period-every-word kind of statements. I do tell a very small collection of people—most of-ten my wife, and one or two others. Let's rewind the clock on our hypothetical goal setting session and change the circumstances to see why.

Whatever drives someone to set a big goal, doing so creates intense emotion, either positive or negative. The hypothetical advisor was feeling on top of the world from her pump-up session. (By the way I often lead those sessions, creating that emotional high and public declaration, so this is really not hypothetical.) What if you have just ex-perienced an emotional low and decide to change something in your life because of the experience? Say you happened to look in the mirror at the ex-act moment you discovered your favorite pants no longer fit, and a whole wave of discontent with your body came crashing down. (This kind of very real non-hypothetical experience has happened to me, so I pick this as an example because many of us may feel the same. Know I am with you!) In that moment you resolve to *DO SOMETHING*. Sign up for the gym, actually use the membership you have paid for since February, start lifting to gain muscle, or start a new eating plan to lose weight. Maybe because of some podcast you just listened to, you get inspired and tell your parents, friends, spouse, and co-workers exactly how quickly you are going to lose 20 pounds. The first couple weeks go amazingly well, you have instant results, and then Shark Week happens.

I mean Shark Week on the Discovery Channel, which means a decrease in gym trips and an increase in popcorn consumption for a week as you take in whatever crazy spectacle they come up with this year. As you backslide in your weight goal, those voices start to creep in, saying things like "my friends acted so nice, but they really knew I couldn't do this, and now they are going to have proof." It is worth repeating: Achieving a new and large goal is really a process of acting like we "remember" ourselves as a person that we have yet to become. This has to be the case, because *if the person that we already are was enough to get the thing we want, we would already have it.* We either don't really want the thing, or we have to become a new person.

That process of remaking or molding ourselves is exactly the same as working out to build new muscle. We tear apart our current selves to force us to grow back bigger and stronger. That is already a painful and risky process, so why the hell would you want to add the stressful risk of letting down the people you love the most, if you could possibly avoid it?

Now Cory, you already told me that you usually tell your wife—aren't you risking letting her down? That's what you're thinking isn't it? If not right now, you would have sooner or later, and I like to get out ahead of potential problems. In my extremely fortunate case, it would be incredibly difficult to let my wife down in this way. I let her down in all kinds of small ways all the time, like forgetting to take the trash out, or forgetting that she only likes white bath towels and giving her light blue ones for her birthday (and for giving my wife bath towels of any kind for her birthday, even really, *really* nice ones). In the larger context of who I am, she is unfailingly supportive. She calls herself my "trailer park wife," because she lived in a double-wide for a period of time as a child (although it was on a California summer camp/horse ranch, so we can hold back the "you poor thing" thoughts). The life we have together has already exceeded both of our expectations for what was possible, so I don't actually have to do much more (besides master the difference between trash, compostable, and recyclable) to keep her happy. That said, I don't admit a goal to her right away.

I do my homework, take a few steps in the right direction, then tell her about the path I am excited to already be completing. You may not have that kind of relationship with your spouse or may not have a spouse, but the point is, find someone who refuses to be let down by you. That is the person you share your goal with first. If you can't find that person in your life, find one person who seems like he might be out to do big things as well, and ask him if he wants to partner with you in holding each other accountable.

When you find your goal setting partner, your job is to portray the new reality that you believe is possible, and present it to him in a way that is believable, despite a current lack of evidence. You have to help him also "remember" the future that you want to create. This is a tall order, and can take a great deal of emotional, mental, and physical energy—another reason not to try to do this with too many people! You need someone in your corner, just don't take too long assembling a team, or you will have no emotional energy left for the actual journey.

Managing your energy inventory along the way is important. Another reason I don't tell a lot of people about my goal is that doing so actually saps the energy needed to produce the outcome. Remember the huge emotional wave (which can be positive or negative) that occurs to get us launched down the path toward a new goal? When you tell someone about your new goal, you get to tell the story of how you created the goal, and your expectations for how amazing life will be when you have achieved it. Every time you retell the amazing story of how you came to launch toward your goal, what is actually going on in your brain is a chemical hit that *simulates the feeling of actually achieving your goal.* Our central nervous systems and the feeling parts of our brains have no concept of past, present, or future. Each time you tell the story of your goal, and how amazing it will be to achieve it, your brain gets a shot of AMAZING-RIGHT-NOW juice. Repeat this several times over, and you slowly fall in love with the *story* of achieving your goal.

Once we fall in love with a story, we tend to want to keep it around. If we actually started *trying*, and fell short of our goal, then not only would we have failed, we would also no longer have the amazing story, doubling our loss. I am willing to bet that you can think of a friend or family member right now who always says, "one day I am going to do _____ and it is going to be awesome!" and has told that same story for years. Told for so many years, and so many re-tellings, in fact, that it has become a living version of the 80s classic movie, *The NeverEnding Story*. Ask yourself, "Where am I telling a NeverEnding Story?"

Some of our friends and family have strong, persistent beliefs about the way we are right now, so it could be difficult for them to change their internal image of you. Some of us have parents or friends who actively try to keep us pressed into the box we occupy in their minds. Many of us just have amazing, loving people in our lives who are all on the same journey of self-discovery that we are. They might be right in the middle of taking their own big leap of faith, and it would be a huge cognitive load for them to have to believe a big unknown about themselves and about you at the same time.

This is because we *all* have our friend the Ego, heavily invested in keeping us exactly the same as we are now. So if you know you have to do battle with your Ego, and your friends and family are doing battle with theirs, can you see why it makes sense to carefully choose who you involve in the early stages of your goal? Think of it like you're staging a surprise birthday party for everyone you know, and you think you can get U2 to perform at the party, but you won't know until the day before. Instead of telling them about U2 on the invitation, and potentially disappointing them, just let it be a surprise, and if U2 doesn't show, your friends still get to have a great party.

Same with a goal—I have told very few friends, family, or colleagues about this book project. In large part because I didn't want to fall in love with the story of writing this book. I am susceptible to flares of pride, and because I have generally been successful in my career and I am an engaging storyteller, telling people about this project was very likely to get them excited, and make me prideful. But that is not why I wrote this book. I didn't want to feed my pride; I wanted to feed my service-driven self that came up with the original idea, in hopes of helping some people create more in their lives and the lives of those they touch. So I committed to a pride-fast, channeled that hunger toward action, and actually worked on the book instead of talking to a lot of people about how good it was going to be.

Furthermore, this project (like most goals) was a fragile newborn baby at the beginning. My vision needed a huge amount of work to become clear, and in the early days I didn't have a lot of conviction around the specifics of the vision, just a general sense of excitement at the big idea. Opening myself to input from a lot of people would have diverted my course at best, and totally stopped my progress at worst.

My recommendation is to find two key people with whom to share your goal. It usually helps to have one person at the same level you are now and one at the level you want to become. Defining how you measure those levels relates to the goal. If you have a business/financial goal, find someone at your level who is also trying to get where you are going, so you can support each other and share the journey. Then find someone at the financial/business level you want to get to, so they can help you understand what that journey looks like.

3. Keep Score

Winners keep score. If you want to win at what you do, keep score. This doesn't mean that you're competing with someone else or trying to push anyone else down. Your Ego is the commissioner of the Complacency League, and not keeping score makes it too easy for your Ego to convince you that you made progress, when you didn't (or the inverse—convincing you you didn't make progress when you did). The first step is to simply write down what you want to happen. This single step alone—simply writing down what you want to accomplish—will immediately improve your results.

A great way to ensure posterity is to write down some objective measures and milestones for our goals. What does "objective measure" mean? Think about a scoreboard: anyone could walk into the arena at any time, and see that one team is clearly and definitively winning, and there would be no way to argue otherwise. Objective measures are specific parameters, usually numbers, that help you know for sure where you stand. The key, then, is not leaving goals and benchmarks up to interpretation. Commit to asking yourself a specific question on a specific date and make sure that the question can only be answered with a yes or no.

Here's a great example:

Did I write 1,000 words for the TPS report over the last week?

However, something like this will not set you up to win:

Did I make good progress on my TPS report?

The Ego always wants to answer yes to the second question, but it has nowhere to hide with the former. "Good progress" could be writing a three sentence outline, "because," the Ego says, "you had a tough week last week. It rained a lot, and you ran out of coffee that one morning, plus you couldn't sleep well Wednesday night, so how could anyone expect you to do better?" The Ego will always rationalize a way to accept excuses, and "rationalize" sounds like "rational-lies."

Creating a time-limited, objective scoreboard for your goal lets the inspired and creative parts of your subconscious get fired up and go to work on your goal for you, processing away even when you are not actively thinking about it. I can't tell you how many times I had a new idea for this book, or a great closing line for a paragraph, pop into my head. First thing in the morning, right as I am going to sleep, during a workout, or in the shower (the greatest thinking space in the modern house). All because I set goals for how much I was going to write along the way, and when I was going to have this book done.

4. Mark the End

In the last section, I mentioned that you should record some milestones for your goal—not just what you hope to accomplish, but when you hope to be finished. Acknowledging the end of a goal period is perhaps the most important step, *especially* if you have not achieved your goal yet. Celebrating failure is even more important than celebrating success. Winning generates an energy all its own, and adding more intentional celebration or bally-hoo on the end is icing on the cake. However, if we don't mark the end of a failed goal, then it quietly sails off into the distance, and in its place the goal leaves behind our old enemy, the Ego. "I told you it wouldn't work out...better luck next time or maybe don't let there be a next time....this always happens when I put myself out there."

Yes, in that last comment, the Ego spoke in the first person, a sneaky trick it uses to convince us that *we* think what *it* thinks *about* us. If we don't mark the end of a goal period, then we get less and less excited and take it less and less seriously each time we have an opportunity to set and pursue a goal.

Celebrating the failure means acknowledging the effort we put forth, identifying what we could have done differently, and finding gratitude for what we learned from the experience. Any failure in which we capture a lesson and take it to our next go-around is actually still moving us closer to our goal. Any time we can fail forward, we aren't really failing at all. Celebrating failure anchors useful feedback from the experience in our memory, so we become more likely to achieve the next goal we set for ourselves.

CHAPTER 4

POWER TOOLS:
LANGUAGE & INTEGRITY

> Language: The User Interface
> Curate Your Language
> Integrity: Your Personal Trust Account
> Components of Trust

Language and integrity are two of the most important tools for building power in our lives. Language creates our picture of the world around us, and integrity creates the picture of us that others see.

Language: The User Interface

In computer operating systems, the user interface is what allows us to interact with all the system's tools and capabilities. In early computers, we used a text-based system that forced the user to enter complicated commands to tell the computer what we wanted it to do. Then came the Graphic User Interface (GUI), which didn't replace those convoluted computer language commands; instead, the GUI linked those commands to specific actions in a virtual landscape—one that replicated tools with which we were accustomed to interacting in the real world.

Thus, Microsoft Windows introduced us to a "desktop" with "files" that we could move into different groups called "folders." Microsoft leveraged the existing meaning we all assigned to those office tools, to create an interface that allowed us interact with the system visually and physically, in an exceptionally intuitive way. For mass adoption, that pre-existing meaning was key. User Interfaces, like jokes, aren't any good if you have to explain them!

In the operating system of our lives, language is the GUI. Language is what allows us to assign meaning to anything, so language is the way we interact with our world. Yes, language is words, but words create images in our mind. Without the language for something, we have a hard time relating to it, or sometimes even seeing it. When European explorers first made contact with the Americas, the large sailing ships moored offshore were "hidden in plain sight" for the native tribes, because they had no language for such a thing.

Think about the answer you would get if you asked a fish, how is the water? Probably something like, "what water?" Language is how we make our way in the world, so it can be easy to take for granted that the language we use has as much impact in creating our thoughts as it does in expressing them.

Like using meditation to separate ourselves from our Ego, the first step toward increasing power through language is to start noticing what we never noticed before. If you can notice your concept of language as a tool apart from yourself, then you can start to find ways to use language to program your life, and stop letting life program you.

Curate Your Language

The thoughts we think impact the way we talk, and the words we speak feed back into our brains to impact the way we think, and the cycle goes on and on.

If we want to change our thoughts and speech patterns, we need to interrupt the cycle from time to time. Since our thoughts are more challenging to control or pin down, and the Ego adds interference, the words we speak are a tangible and actionable way to drive change in our lives. By curating your language, you can create immediate change. One example is the words *should* versus *could*.

Picture a lazy Sunday afternoon. There is a donut sitting there on the counter, and on the floor below it, your gym bag. You haven't worked out all weekend. You tell yourself "I *should* go to the gym," and as the guilt racks your system, you devour the donut, repeating in your mind "I really *should* go to the gym," further reinforcing the guilt and negativity that you now associate with working out.

Using the word should often transforms the conversation into a moral construct of right or wrong, when that is often not the context in which we make a decision. Many of the choices we face are actually questions of workability, not morality. In the case of gym versus donut, the more effective self-talk is: I *could* go to the gym, or I *could* eat this donut. Now we avoid setting off a guilt-ridden chain reaction of self-destruction, and are more likely to engage in a balanced evaluation of what activity produces the outcome we are after. Now that you will notice the difference, you will be amazed at how often you are should-ing all over yourself and the people in your life.

Another example is *but* versus *and*. How many times have we all said phrases like: "I love you, but...", or, "that is a great idea, but..." You know you have—we all have! So what is the problem? Any sentiment we express in the first half of the sentence is negated by that giant BUT! How many fights with a significant other have started because of a misplaced "but"? Instead, try AND. "I love you, and..." creates both a clear and positive tone, even if the rest of the sentence is constructively critical.

In a work setting, phrases like, "I like your idea, BUT I think we should do _____ differently" come up a lot. What that actually says to someone is, "I like your idea, but I just lied about that first part of the sentence, I think your idea is stupid, except for this one part that I alone can salvage, and here is how I would make it better." In our polite society, we are trained to find ways to politely fight with people. What kind of roadblocks might exist in your relationships from politely telling people over and over that they are wrong? Especially in the local passive-aggressive culture we Seattleites love to grumble about, there are lots of situations where no one would even consciously realize what just happened, but we internalize feelings of marginalization, and they subtly eat away at relationships like termites. "I like your idea AND I think we should do _____ differently" shows respect for someone else, and allows you to express an alternative view both authentically and openly.

Integrity: Your Personal Trust Account

If we are going to make any kind of significant impact in the world, we will require a large network of help, other humans with whom we build strong trust and on whom we can depend to produce predictable results. The only way to build trust is to always act with integrity. Not integrity in the moral sense, but like the integrity that keeps a table standing—structural integrity.

The first person to convince of your own integrity is yourself. This is so important because you need trust yourself in order to enable others to trust you. Once you start trusting yourself, you start moving with the world in a more powerful way—a way that makes it easier for other people to trust you. Every day you either build a trust account with thousands of tiny deposits, or your trust dies a slow and painful death by a thousand cuts. Showing up a few minutes late to a meeting, not calling when you said you would, last minute cancellations—no single one of these events is going to make or break trust, AND it is amazing how quickly a negative body of proof can compound from just a few examples.

That is why I constantly seek out ways to prove that what I say comes true. I text when I think I will be five minutes late to a "come at 6:00ish" dinner invitation. Sometimes the response is "Okay crazy, see you when you get here, we are just sitting around having a beer, no rush." Yet I know that I am adding another deposit to the relationship bank each time I do something like that. Over time an unstated idea forms: "If Cory is this particular about something so small as a five-minute delay in arriving for dinner, he must be amazingly rigorous and out-of-this-world dependable about something that actually matters."

Components of Trust

Trust is a near magical commodity. We can create or destroy it at the speed of light, and it can act as a catalyst for creating amazing value between people. In organized society, we all share a baseline of trust, like the unspoken agreement that we can all safely drive down the road and people going the opposite direction won't cross the thin white line. Clearly that is a different kind of trust than a parent might have in someone he allows to care for his baby. Any time we develop a relationship with someone else, we build or destroy trust through four key elements. I call them the Component Proofs.

The **Four Components Proofs of Trust** are:

Sincerity: Do you mean what you say?
Reliability: Can you follow through on what you said?

Knowledge: Do you have the skills to do what you said?
Alignment: Does what you want align with what they want?

Let's break those down a little further:

Sincerity measures whether we mean what we say. When I say we should hang out, and you say sure, we should do that some time, do you really mean it, or you are just saying yes to avoid an uncomfortable moment in the conversation? Sincerity is really Integrity by another name. I think we all know the person who says yes to everything, with no thought as to whether they actually can or want to follow through. Don't be that person.

Reliability measures your operational ability to follow through. We all have friends to whom we give a start time 30 minutes ahead of when we actually want to meet, to make sure they are there on time. We know they are sincere when they say they will meet us, we just know they won't run their life in a way to reliably get there on time. If none of your friends come to mind as that person, consider that you might be that person in your group.

Knowledge looks at your technical ability to pull off the desired outcome. Even if I can demonstrate that I sincerely care about someone, and can reliably do what I say I will do, no one that knows me would accept my offer to perform any kind of surgery on them, because I don't have that skill or experience. In fact, if I even made the offer to perform surgery, my nonchalance would almost certainly drive that person to reevaluate my Sincerity and Reliability—proof that all the component truths are interdependent, feeding off of one another.

Alignment measures motivation. For all of the previous three to really matter, you need to see that my interests align with your interests in what we are both trying to accomplish. The best kind of alignment comes from a sense of selfish altruism. Selfish altruism means you are doing the best for me because it is also the best for you, which is the kind of motivation with the longest legs. Pure altruism only goes so far, because as humans we all need to eat at the end of the day. I am sure you have experienced a person who approaches you with so much apparent selfless good intention that you instantly become suspicious. If I know that you know that what is best for me is also what is best for you, then we are locked in on a great path together.

The *Four Component Proofs* are not a magic spell to instantly get anyone to trust you. They *are* a guide to continually demonstrating trustworthiness, and a checklist to help you avoid eroding trust over time. Sincerity and Reliability take time to build with someone else, and they must be built in advance of your need to rely on them. Knowledge takes time for you to build personally, however, it can be outsourced. If you can demonstrate

Sincerity and Reliability, it's a whole lot easier for someone who trusts you to more quickly trust an expert that you vouch for. That's what happens when you make or receive a professional introduction. And once the other three elements are in place, Alignment can be quickly established.

If you are early in your career, knowledge can't yet be a competitive advantage for you, although leaning into the gap with determination can change that quickly. In the meantime, language and integrity are two great tools for gaining traction. If you are later in your career, or in the midst of reinventing yourself, then your knowledge is a huge asset, and your language and integrity are the best tools you have to make people care about what you know.

If you are afraid that you might start speaking in a way that doesn't sound quite like you, then you are actually on the right path. If you want people to think about you differently than they have in the past, to treat you differently, then you are going to have to *be* different than you have been in the past. Once you get their attention with words, watch what happens when you actually follow through with the actions to match. It is both a sad commentary on modern culture and an exciting opportunity: people whose words and actions align are incredibly rare. Start being someone who actually does what you say you are going to do, and suddenly you'll find yourself with a priceless competitive advantage.

CHAPTER 5

GAMES OF POWER

- ➤ Whose Game Are You Playing?
- ➤ Creating Games
- ➤ My Favorite Application of True vs. Useful
- ➤ Playing Games, Not Gaming Others

Games! In the 80s and 90s, every teen and tween already knew that games were the real reason computers were invented. Business spreadsheets and homework were the justification for getting computers into our homes; games were the reason. Want proof? Many computers invented over time *only* play games—Pong, Atari, Gameboy, and Nintendo 64—but has there ever, in all of history, been a work-only computer that couldn't play a game of some kind? Even a basic calculator, a most primitive computer, lets us write funny upside down messages to our friends. Games and the concept of play are indelibly written into our nature, so anything we create has the potential to facilitate a game.

I freely admit to you that I am a gamer. My generation is not the first to grow up with video games, but we are the first to continue to regard video games as a legitimate hobby as we reach adulthood. With the advent of mobile gaming, all of our mothers (many of whom frequently beseeched us to stop playing our "silly games" in our teen years) joined us as gamers when they became at least temporarily addicted to something like Words with Friends or Bejeweled, maybe even Angry Birds. Most living adults have now experienced that dopamine hit of finishing a level, beating back the zombies, or some other game-winning task that doesn't actually produce anything except a warm fuzzy feeling.

When we play a game, we have clear rules, and frequent feedback on success or failure. Gamification is a growing trend, where mundane or unpleasant tasks are overlaid with some kind of game component to make the experience more enjoyable. Pokemon Go was a flash-flood phenom that made walking outside fun for the pasty-faced crowd simply by splashing pictures of cute creatures on smartphone cameras. The much more permanent Geocaching phenomenon turns urban and wild landscapes into a vast real-life treasure map. The gamification concept goes all the way back to typing tutor programs that moved a character through levels as the player increased the speed and accuracy of his typing skills. The elements of a game that draw us in are clear rules, regular positive feedback, and a lack of fear at the outcome.

My wife and I took a vacation to Hawaii during her Spring Break from Medical School, and we had a great time stepping out of day-to-day life for a spell. As we were flying back home after our week away, we both realized we were as excited to go home as we had been to leave on the trip. (Give me a little creative license, ok, no one is truly excited to leave Hawaii.) In the midst of our conversation, Danielle said something that gave me a whole new perspective. She said, "we are going back to our long games." That's when the realization hit me: I could put myself in a position to experience even greater fulfillment, adrenaline, and level-beating satisfaction, by creating amazing games in my everyday life. Games that don't have flashing lights and imaginary weapons, and instead help me achieve my highest-reaching goals.

Whose Game Are You Playing?

Whether we love video games, board games, or neither, we all play games every day of our lives, *and if we haven't intentionally chosen our own game, we are playing someone else's.* Others' games might be fine for a time, and the objectives might overlap nicely with yours, but in many cases playing someone else's game moves you toward *their* desired result and away from your own. This makes identifying the current games in your life a critical first step. If you don't know what game you are currently playing, then how could you possibly be sure that you are playing the right one?

We are frequently pulled into other people's games, and sometimes that is okay. Every winning presidential candidate only got to the White House because he enrolled just enough people to play in a game called "my vision for the country," and all those people only played the game because they saw how the President's game aligned with their own interests. The problem is when we unwittingly enter into games that hurt us, or rob us of the chance to win the games we would really rather be playing.

Creating Games

Every piece of significance or meaning is invented. We either play by someone else's (or society's) rules that we have adopted, or we create our own. Any meaning we perceive comes out of language we use to describe it. In fact, without language, we would have no way to ascribe meaning to anything. And if we invent the meaning behind our situation using language, then we can choose the language that helps us create useful meaning for the games we play every day.

The key here is to construct a game around our life goals. Can we turn the process of pounding out TPS Reports into a mesmerizing and wonderful Super Mario World experience? Maybe not—at least not until virtual reality makes some giant leaps. What we can do, however, is realize that we created all the dreadful significance of the world around us, no different than game designers defining the rules and objectives in the worlds they build. You're not going to turn every boring TPS Report into a magical fantasy land, but picture thinking about life more like a game. With a little imagination and some strategic language, every TPS report, every strategy meeting, every hard-earned paycheck, is one dragon slayed (or Pac-Man ghost eaten) in your quest to achieve the life you desire. Yes, it sounds a little silly, and that is exactly my point. If every paycheck you cash makes you think of accumulating gold to buy a better piece of magical armour, hopefully you chuckle to yourself every time you go to the bank, and hopefully that helps you take life a little less seriously.

In high school I spent tireless hours in game worlds, figuring out puzzles or mastering patterns to push through opponents. The key to my stamina was twofold: engagement, and a dismissal of fear. In a game world we feel free to try out new solutions, and fail (aka die!) over and over again, because we know there is always a do-over. And unless we find ourselves in a physical life-or-death situation, life almost always gives us do-overs. Real-life failures might not loop us back to start again at exactly the same place. We might not get a second shot at *the* job we wanted after falling flat in the interview, but there are always more interviews. Our real life do-overs are going to look different each time, but they will always come along, as long as we keep playing the game.

Games help us detach ourselves from hanging on to a specific result at a specific time (which we can't control anyway), and focus on our current action instead. Focusing on action over end results tends to improve the result in the end, and that is really the point of all games—take the player out of her head, and help her dive unreservedly into a world where she can be anything she wants to be.

My Favorite Application of
True vs. Useful

Games have a defined set of rules, which often cause us to behave differently than we would in regular life. No one necessarily assigns meaning to the rules of a game, they just are. Never have I witnessed anyone being accused of lying while reading the rules of Monopoly. I have tried making up rules, sure, but the rule book itself is not "true" or "false"—it just is what it is. People play Charades and start acting in ways they never would normally, yet everyone on their team is okay with it, because the circumstances are declared and understood by all involved, and the behavior moves them all toward a common objective.

In real life, we can experience huge breakthroughs when we play for higher stakes than Charades, and can get other people to join our new and outrageous games. Steve Jobs started a game called "my computer should just work," and lots of people joined in. He then created other games, like "my phone should be more than a phone." Apple became one of the most successful companies ever, and in the process Steve Jobs changed the world.

The first step in training your brain is to create and play games that only you know about. This is particularly helpful in managing mood and our reactions to events. Since we have no control over what happens to us, managing how powerfully we can respond to events is the only way we can really make progress. These kinds of games don't have to have defined rules or even make much sense. Their real function is awareness and mood management. Playing a game called "How many times can I get someone to say no to my offer" is about recontextualizing negative emotions around getting turned down on the road toward getting a yes. Just the act of setting something as a game helps us take it less seriously, paradoxically helping us doing better at it. Hell, the only way I got this book done was to start playing a fantasy game called "being an author," enabling me to suspend disbelief until that fantasy became reality.

Playing a Game, NOT Gaming Other People

Game Theory is the scientific study of games. Yes, this kind of science could turn fun into boring real fast, but it gives us a useful way to define some basic types of games. Games that end in a win/win are called Positive Sum games, because if my record goes up by one (+1) and so does yours, then the sum of 1+1 is positive. Games where one person wins and the other person loses are called "zero sum" games, because if I end at a +1 and you leave with a -1, then the total real value we have created = 0. Negative

Sum games occur when everybody loses by playing, like a nuclear war, or setting a new record for most people doing the macarena at once.

Any game that doesn't also create value for the other participants is a zero sum game. Even a game that seems like it is neither helping nor hurting the other person is actually a negative to them, simply because we all have limited time in our lives, so any experience that doesn't add value actually incurs the cost of a missed opportunity.

Ponzi scheme. The long con. An illicit affair. These are all games that people play without properly enrolling all the participants, and without a view to creating value for everyone involved. Bernie Madoff created an investment firm in the 1960s, that may or may not have been legitimate at the beginning. All we know for sure is that by somewhere in the 1980s or 1990s, the majority of his business was a Ponzi scheme, where he used money from new investors and falsified reporting to create the illusion of growth for current investors. At first this created profit for Madoff and loss for his customers, so it seemed like a zero sum game: +1 Bernie, -1 customers. Then in 2008, Madoff's sons, whom he had hired into the business along with his brother Peter, released news that their father had confessed his long-term scheme to them. What followed was the family's complete and total collapse. Bernie in jail for life, Peter for 10 years, both sons dead—one of suicide, one of cancer.

Madoff was accused of false dealing in the past, so his confession may have been the result of a guilty conscience, or may have been forced upon him by inevitability of such a giant fraud coming to light. Either way, Madoff's story shows that all games are either positive or negative sum. There is no neutral when when it comes to value; we either create it or erode it. Make sure you always create valuable games, otherwise the only person you're gaming is yourself.

CHAPTER 6

SOCIAL POWER

➤ Crafting Your Identity
➤ Communicate More Powerfully
➤ Speak Your Moods
➤ Make Awkward Parties Amazing

Crafting Your Identity

As children, we encounter a critical paradox. The first time you faced it, you probably didn't even realize it was a paradox. Early in our primary school career, we get teased for a part of our personality that is different from those around us, and our moms comfort us by saying something along the lines of "just be yourself, don't worry about what other people think." This is great advice, because living our lives to please other people (especially the kind of people who would criticize you simply for being who you are) is no way to live. But, here is the paradox: We shouldn't live our lives for the approval of the world, AND we need other people's cooperation to build the life we want to live. So how do we reconcile the paradox? By crafting an identity.

Think of this like building your BitMoji or a new character profile in a video game. Who do you want to be to the world? It is all well and good for our moms to tell us not to care what other people think, yet I know that as a financial advisor, it's important to my community that I demonstrate some basic, but specific, qualities and capabilities.

In the mid to late 1990s, Dennis Rodman became a fixture in Chicago sports, as much for his rebounding and defensive performance on the basketball court as for his general theatrics both on and off the court. Chicago fans all eagerly waited to see how he would color his hair next, and what crazy off-the-court antics he would get into. My favorite was when he tried to marry himself, even going so far as to put on a wedding dress. Rodman could be this crazy because his behavior didn't detract from his ability to be excellent at his day job, basketball, and didn't detract from his team's ability to count on him on the basketball court. His antics may have in fact *enhanced* his on-court performance, because an opponent who knew how crazy Rodman was off the court might think it likely that Rodman could snap on the court and go crazy on him.

Because I advise people on important life decisions and strategies, I know I can't act as crazy as Dennis Rodman and be successful, not with the kind of people that I want to work with. Even if I wanted to work solely with people like Dennis Rodman (I don't), I suspect I would still have to act like an anchored, responsible person. Behind closed doors, Rodman would probably say, "I love being crazy, and I need a non-crazy person looking at my money so I can keep being crazy." In my own community, I need to come across as stable and predictable, so people know that they can count on me.

The difference between living your life based on other's opinions, and "crafting your identity" is intention. Crafting your identity starts with you planning whom you want to be in the world, to occupy the niche that you want to carve out, and slowly building a case that you are who you say you are.

The good news, and possibly the challenge, is you have been building this case your whole life. It is good news if you have been acting in a way that creates corroborating evidence for who you want to be. However, you may face a challenge if you have been demonstrating to the world a different person than you really want to be now. Just like planting a tree, the best time to build your identity is 20 years ago...or *right now*. If re-crafting your identity is necessary, find someone with a similar reputation to that which you desire, and start acting as if you already had the reputation they enjoy.

Often the most difficult, and always the most crucial person to convince of our new identity is ourselves. Our Ego constantly tells us that we are the way we are now for a reason, and we should stay the way we are, so it is critical to build an air-tight case to start proving to ourselves that we can grow into that new identity.

Here are some ways that we build a case for an identity we probably don't want, every single day:

Being late: Every time we are late, we say to everyone else: my time is more important than your time. Whatever else I was doing, or whoever else I was talking to is more important, and I don't think highly enough of you to tell you I am changing the deal we had made; I am just going to let the time you reserved for me go to waste.

Breaking commitments: This is a variation on being late. Canceling last minute is saying exactly the same thing as being late, with an added asterisk: "I suddenly found something I would rather be doing, and the feeling I get from doing that thing is more important to me than the relationship I have with you." Reversing course on this one practice alone could produce a huge breakthrough in your life.

Talking behind others' backs: People instinctively know the Principle of Consistency: how you are anywhere = how you are everywhere. When we speak about another person to our friend, that friend is at least subconsciously processing the fact that we are likely to be saying things to other people about them.

I know we all have times when something actually did happen out of our control. Maybe we got sick to a point that we would literally be worse than useless if we heaved ourselves into the car and actually showed up. Just honestly ask yourself what your ratio of genuine to disingenuous cancellations or late arrivals is.

The next question to ask is: What if we got really *un*reasonable, and started a radical commitment to keeping commitments? My goal is to create an identity where people believe in my near wizard-like powers in keeping commitments. I need this to be the case so that when I tell a client or an employee that I am going to do something, they walk away from that conversation already believing that the future I promised is going to become real. If that is true about me, then I am someone who can be counted on at a high level, and if I can be counted on at a high level, then I can work with amazing high-level people to produce incredible new realities in their lives.

In order to cultivate that kind of identity, I generally can't get into the kind of crazy antics that Dennis Rodman did. So I do care very much what other people think of me, but I care what they think of me in relation to the person I have chosen to be. That is the solution to the identity paradox.

Enhancing Communication

Social media is both a help and a hindrance to true communication. Once upon a time we had to be in the same room as each person with whom we hoped to speak. Then we could write letters and trade messages from afar, over the course of weeks or months. Then we could send telegrams, and then make phone calls, which was much faster, yet we were still primarily communicating one-on-one. When I was in middle school, AOL Instant Messenger let me talk to as many of my closest friends as I wanted, all at the same time! At my peak I had five or six conversations going at once.

These days, quantity of communication has reached fever pitch—we can send more words, pictures, and videos to more people at any one time than ever before. It strikes me that many non-famous and semi-famous individuals probably have a greater audience with each tweet than many major television broadcasts in the early sixties. What we missed along the way was equal development in the *skill* with which we communicate, or the quality of our interactions. As you seek to communicate more effectively and powerfully, you could ask yourself one key question before any important conversation. This question applies to any type of conversation, and becomes more and more important as you enter higher stakes conversations:

What result would I most want to produce in this conversation?

Say you have a roommate, or a significant other, who is supposed to take out the trash. You are the first to arrive home after work one evening, and the trash is sitting in the kitchen, overflowing from a bag bulging past capacity. The worst part is, you specifically reminded him to take the trash out that morning (the second time you reminded him), and he had reaffirmed that he would complete his chore.

You spend the remaining 30 minutes before he arrives at home developing a creatively clever and devastatingly delicious diatribe filled with righteous indignation at his complete lack of responsibility and other general shortcomings as a human being. Oh boy, are you going to get him good!

Does this scenario sound like one in which *anyone* will actually win? We all know that no one will, because we have all been there. Whether it was in a roommate/spouse situation, or with a sibling, parent, best friend, etc, we have all had someone we care about let us down in some way. Even though the names and places in my story have been changed to protect the innocent, the scenario has played itself out the same way in all of our lives.

What we really need to ask ourselves before launching down a deliciously derisive path is: "what do I really want to have happen from this conversation?" If the goal is to produce a short term emotional release and the satisfaction of a delicious moment, then we can very easily win that little game and lose at a much bigger and more important game.

I have struggled with this distinction for a long time. My Ego believes I am very often right in an objective sense. I still have to remind myself that the "perfect perspective" is a definition I created, that others may not share. Especially my wife. I have always had a natural gift for logical argument, which combines with my aforementioned confidence in my beliefs, to give me an amazing gift for being, on occasion, an incredibly frustrating person to be around, because I can almost always find a way to rationalize the "rightness" of my view.

When you find yourself in your own version of that tough conversation, think about a bigger and deeper goal than feeling good or right in the moment. Even for something as simple as a conversation about the temperature in the room, it's important to remember that we each live in a reality created by our feelings. If you feel it is too cold, and

I feel it is too hot, who is right doesn't really matter. We are both the sovereign ruler of our own reality around temperature. And we are both right! Since there is no objective truth when comparing your feelings to someone else's, take yourself out of the game of justification. There is an even bigger and more rewarding game out there called "creating workability in the relationship."

In every single conversation with my wife, the game I want to play is one of strengthening our relationship and making our lives work. The more I can dwell on what is workable for her, the better I can find a situation that is also workable for me. We continually remind each other that we are on the same team, and starting there makes it much easier to create workability together.

This doesn't only work with husbands and wives. Being on the same team can be valuable in any kind of conversation. By simply asking, "in what way could we (you and the other person) end up on the same team" or, "what team could we both play on and both win," you can open up so many amazing possibilities. For an unhelpful customer service representative (another situation we all face in our lives), you could invent a team called "two mutually respectful and valuable human beings conversing openly." If you want to instantly double the pleasantness of your experiences with customer service representatives, start playing a game called "being the most memorably human and humane person they have talked to all day." Since customer service calls typically end with stressed out people on both ends of the line, just by being a shining bright spot in their day you will instantly increase the likelihood that they will go out of their way to make magic happen in fulfilling your request.

Speak Your Moods

Another tool for relationship building is the Declaration of Moods. The first big caveat is that the degree of personal disclosure should necessarily vary in proportion to the degree of intimacy we share with the person with whom we are interacting. This can be an amazingly effective tool in talking to even complete strangers, just don't weird them out by going too deep down the emotional well.

A mood is any pre-existing fog of emotion through which we filter our communication, both in how we speak, and how we hear others speak to us. Moods can be positive or negative. No conversation occurs in a vacuum. In all cases, both parties bring a pre-existing atmosphere to the interaction—the sum total of all the decisions we have made about how to think about and react to everything that has happened to us before coming into the current conversation.

Many times we're still in the middle of processing feelings from a prior interaction, so our reactions to the person in front of us may not be all about that person. By declaring our moods, we can often dissolve them, because voicing the mood helps suck the life out of it. I might have had the most amazing day and come home supercharged on life, leaving Danielle surprised and confused at why I am suddenly rearranging all the furniture in our house and attempting to reoptimize everything in five minutes. Speaking our moods gives the other person a powerful lens through which to view our words and actions, and the more we speak our own moods, the more we develop a sense for the moods of others. Our listening and response can become more effective over time, too, even without hearing a declaration of mood from the other person.

Understanding mood filters is a big win, because you will react less strongly when someone becomes a less-than-amazing conversation partner with you. An angry co-worker does not usually draw the full source of his anger from you, but from his kids, partner, or boss. When someone else comes at you with an external mood blowing at gale force speeds, doing nothing more than coming from a place of understanding and not reacting or rising to the level of their mood can be better for both of you.

Here is an example: Danielle and I were talking, making plans for the weekend. On this particular Wednesday or Thursday, I was listless and non-committal about deciding what to do. I am very often quick and decisive in making plans, so Danielle was soon frustrated, especially because we were trying to plan a date night, and she is (rightfully) accustomed to being my favorite person to make plans with. I realized that I was not being a particularly great conversation partner, and that my distance in conversation was creating distance between us in the moment. I really *was* excited about having a free day coming up, for us to spend time together, especially because date night had become a rare occurrence since she started medical school. The real reason for my ennui: I had a few difficult conversations at work earlier in the day, with one person in particular frustrating me so much that I couldn't focus my mind on anything besides the problem. I realized I was bringing those feelings into my mood as I interacted with Danielle. So I spoke my mood: "I am really excited about doing a date this weekend, and right now I am being grouchy because I am dwelling on my frustration with this person at work today."

A powerful transformation occurred in that moment. Danielle gained both affirmation of our relationship, and a new context through which she could view my bad behavior and assign motivations for that behavior other than her. That doesn't mean she was instantly happy about everything, or that she excused my behavior. But once Danielle knew that the source of my behavior was not her or her actions, she had the opportunity (which she thankfully accepted) to draw new territorial boundaries in the conversation, with the two of us on one side, and this problem of my mood sitting alone on the other.

You will also find, like I did, that declaring the reason for a bad mood tends to dissipate it. As soon as I declared my mood to Danielle, I then had to ask myself: "Why am I grouchy toward my wife, my favorite human, because of an earlier interaction with someone I don't like much at all?" In that moment I had to laugh. Hearing the reason out loud (even "out loud" in my head) helped me see how silly it was to be grouchy around her because of a situation from the past. My mood lifted instantly.

Speaking mood works with non-intimate conversation as well. Take customer service representatives again: Many people they talk to only call because they are upset about some kind of problem or situation that the rep did not create, and is only trying to help solve. Yet many people talk to service reps like that person on the phone has fatally wounded them personally. When I need to call customer service, and find myself especially upset about a problem, I typically start out the call with something like this: "Look, I am upset about X, and I know that you didn't have anything to do with that personally, so please know, if I sound upset as we talk, I am not mad at you." Start with this narrative and continue the conversation with the "mutual human" game from a few pages back, and you will likely experience better outcomes because you are helping both people in the conversation win! Again, no magic spells here. Some situations just won't work out in your favor, and if you continually give yourself at least the opportunity to turn your most stressful moments into victories, a profoundly positive change will occur, as the sum total of all your conversations over time.

Make Awkward Parties Amazing

Every human over the age of 12 has walked into a room of other people and felt unsure of himself. How do some people seem to effortlessly float into a party and own the room? Some are born with a natural lack of self-consciousness that lends itself to amazing results in large social settings. Others have developed strategies to overcome fear and convince themselves that they are not self-conscious. Either way, the ultimate goal is to get out of our own heads and have a plan. Large gatherings of people will happen over and over in your life, and they are often opportunities to meet new people with influence. Few of us can be the effortless, lamp-shade-on-the-head, life-of-the-party-person, however, all of us can become the kind of valuable addition to an event that makes hosts want to keep inviting us back.

The first shift (and for some already outgoing people, the only one they will need) is to enter every party with the mindset that you are the host, here to make sure that everyone has a great time. Don't start ordering around the waitstaff, or cutting a cake that has yet to be served, just survey the landscape, looking for any stranded guests. Have you ever stood awkwardly alone in an island of silence watching other groups of people talk?

Would you have welcomed someone's offer of rescue from that purgatory? *So would everyone else!* Here is a secret: There is no master club of people who meet to decide who is going to talk to whom parties. The surest way to rescue yourself from a lonely island is to become the rescuer. Just start walking around at a moderate but purposeful pace (another great technique to calm yourself at parties) until you spot someone who looks like they need rescuing from being alone.

As you approach, you have to be ready to break the ice. You don't need to explain why you walked up to them—you are already at a party, talking to people is the point. You do want to have something to talk about though. The good news is you can rehearse this opening line far in advance. In fact, I recommend practicing and committing to memory your five or six favorite conversation starters, so you have an opener and several backups in case you require conversational life support.

Questions like "How are you?" or "How you been?" are the conversational equivalent of a doctor checking a patient's vitals. We say those words just to make sure the other person is really alive. The question is automatic and rote, and that is the exact kind of answer all of us give and get to those kinds of questions. Questions like, "What's new?" end up with an answer like "not much" over 90% of the time. What we need are powerful questions that require the other person to tell a story to answer. Once someone else starts telling a story, you are going to think of a story of your own halfway through theirs, and then the conversation starts to take on a life of its own. So go into the fray with your favorite five or six questions ready in advance, and feel free to reuse them with every new person or group you talk with at your event. Here are some of my favorites of the moment.

The Lead In: Always approach with a smile, right hand slowly extending for a shake, as you say: "Hi, I'm Cory" (of course your own name for any of you jokers out there). "My Name Is _____" was the phrase that 1990s telemarketers used to introduce themselves, and a time machine is the only place we should find those words today.

Now, for your starters:

The Mundane

1. So how do you know _____ (host of party)?

2. I just wanted to say, those are some great _____(insert article of clothing or jewelry).

3. How do you like the _____ (food that they are eating as you walk up)?

    (*Advantage to this question: If you want a quick exit, you can say "Well then, I am going to grab some of those meatballs!"*)

4. Hi there, I don't know a lot of people here tonight, so I thought I would introduce myself.

(If you are at a friend's house for a party, eye contact is the only excuse needed to simply start introducing yourself. After all, everyone is there to be social, and by introducing yourselves, you help your friend the host have a better party.)

The Daring
(You may consider a lead-in comment like, "I'm working on avoiding small talk, so I have a fun question for you, is that okay?")

1. What is something, big or small, that you are passionate about right now?

2. Tell me something awesome. What is your favorite thing that happened last week?

3. What has surprised you recently?

Avoid If Possible

1. Weather

2. Traffic (Especially which route you took to get there.)

These can feel like safe fall back topics, but they are the most meaningless kind of filler. At best a very boring person will be comfortable talking to you. At worst, a very interesting person will find you incredibly boring. (One major exception here is my friend and editor Karen Quinn, who is fascinated by the weather. The lesson here is really "read your audience.")

All of these questions are impossible to answer with "yes," "no," "not much," or "good." They also encourage a positive conversation. Nothing drains your social energy faster than sticking yourself with someone who just launched into complaint mode. Fair warning: some people will be so thrown off by someone showing actual interest in them, that they may freeze up with no answer. In those situations they will often throw the question back to you—have an answer ready for your own question!

Are you reading this thinking that such a pre-meditated approach to conversation feels disingen-uous? I have gotten that before. While I don't go into every single social encounter with a twelve-point plan, I do tend to dedicate a lot of my background processing and day-dreaming to storing up poten-tial conversation situations. That is only because I really enjoy talking to people and care about them having a good time when they talk to me. If being intentional about planning conversation feels some-how fake, then wouldn't taking it to the extreme oth-er end of the spectrum mean that not caring about relationship and leaving everything to chance is the most noble thing to do? I don't think so.

Finally, to really arm yourself with courage going in, you need an exit plan at the ready, to help each of you move on gracefully when the conversation has run its course. The surest way for you to try my advice once and throw away my book immediately afterward is to attempt to rescue someone from a lonely island and end up getting stranded there for the whole party. The greatest awkwardness in human existence is two awkward people with nothing more to say to each other, who also have no idea how to break away. Here are some ways:

Easy

"Well it was great to talk to you, I am going to go refill my drink, enjoy the party!"

(Caveat: If they seem to be enjoying the conversation much more than you, they might not get the hint, and may in fact follow you to the punchbowl.)

Moderate:

"Hey it has been great talking with you, and I don't want to take all of your time. "

Another handshake is a good physical accompaniment to signal the end of the conversation.

Advanced:

If you can sense a natural denouement to the conversation, just a quick pat on the arm, a short handshake, and a "good to talk to you," can be a very graceful way out for both of you.

CHAPTER 7

PRODUCTIVE POWER

➤ Myth of Linear Thinking
➤ Billing $1,000 an hour
➤ Quitting Toward Success
➤ Just Beat Zero: How Propinquity Trumps Entropy

Productivity. Productive. These words and all the derivations thereof are their own culture in our society. They are not so much words anymore, as they are an atmosphere. A fish doesn't define water, and neither do we stop to define productivity—we simply swim through it as quickly as possible.

There are lots books out there about how to get more tasks done in less time, which has become the default definition of productivity. In an assembly line or most other manual labor, "do more in less time" is mostly effective, although if a worker makes an hourly wage, then he may not be incentivized to complete *the most* work in a given shift, but rather to complete *just enough* to keep that hourly wage coming in.

Apps like Uber, Instacart, and PostMates are part of the "gig economy," where individuals are rewarded for completing individual tasks, incentivizing them to complete more tasks in less time. However, this behavior is not entirely innate. Classic economics predicts that humans always behave "rationally," making the best choice to maximize their own interests. This assumes that we have enough information to fully evaluate our decisions. A classic blunder for Uber drivers is to work less when demand is high (aka, prices have surged) and work more when ride requests are low (prices falling). Rationally, the most effective behavior would be to work as long as possible when the payoff is the best, and take the day off or find more valuable work when rates are low.

What classic economics misses, and the now maturing field of behavioral economics seeks to understand better, is human interference, as with our old friend the Ego. What we find with new Uber drivers is that they sign up to drive with an income goal in mind—usually a number designed to meet their current monthly expenses. That number makes the Ego feel safe, usually because the number is achievable, and risk of failure is low. So when prices surge and ride requests are high, the driver gets there faster, and finishes up earlier. When traffic is slow, he sticks with it until he reaches that same number, leading to a longer day. Thus, maximizing productivity is a lot more complex when we consider human behavior as part of the equation.

In the knowledge work world, where our output comes from our minds rather than our hands, the quest for productivity is all but unquenchable. Most work-related cultural beliefs are rooted in the Industrial Revolution—values like "the importance of hard work," or "be the first to arrive and the last to leave," or "a fair day's wage for a fair day's work," are left over from a time when most of us earned a living by being in a specific place for a specific amount of time, moving some physical output toward completion.

The key to making a huge leap in productivity is not learning how to work harder. Consider someone making $100,000/year as a freelance writer, working 60 hours a week to finish all the projects needed to get to that income. If we then met a freelance writer making $200,000/year, is it physically possible for the second writer to be making twice the income by applying double the brute-force effort? Of course not. Whether you define productivity as making more money, doing more tasks, or helping more people, increased force is not the answer.

The Myth of Linear Thinking

At the root of the problem is a reliance on linear-based thinking, and pulling ourselves out of this frame of mind is not easy. After all, language (that persistent User Interface!) drilled into us from child-hood is reinforces linear thinking. "The shortest distance between two points is a straight line" comes from math class; in English we read novels from beginning to end; and in life in general, we are taught "if at first you don't succeed, try try again," meaning we start along a path and we are taught that it is bad to stop before we reach the end. There is a lot of value in not giving up easily, yet what if we defined differently that which we were giving up?

Vilfredo Pareto was an Italian economist who observed, in the late 1800s, that 20% of the citizens of Italy owned 80% of the land. Then he also noticed that 80% of the peas from his garden were coming from 20% of the peapods. This disproportionate relationship between input and output is known as Pareto's principle, and while it is not a hard physical constant like the law of gravity, it does illustrate the persistent truth that most of our results come from a small proportion of our activities.

Here's another example, from the stock market: Many people understand the general principle that over the long term, investing in markets tends to produce positive growth or rate of return (ROR). What we generally leave out is the nature and timing of the accrual of those returns. In the following chart, you can see a summary of 20 years of results in the S&P 500 index, from July 1, 1993 to June 30th, 2013, for a total of 5,040 trading days. *(NOTE: I feel compelled to request that you not take this as any kind of financial advice. This is not meant to suggest how, if, or when, you should invest in the stock market. There is a lot more to the story than this chart!)*

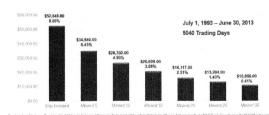

Simply putting money into the index on day one, completely ignoring the investment, and coming back to check 20 years later would produce an annual average ROR of 8.66% (before taxes to the government or fees to a financial institution or advisor). In the following columns we can see the resulting ROR after missing the highest individual days of return in that period. In the third column, we can see that missing just the 10 best days of growth out of 5,040 or .0019% of days, delivered 58% less return than all of the days. Clearly the disproportion in this example is much greater than the 80/20 that Pareto observed.

Technology is changing our world economy, ushering in a new reality where unskilled labor is replaced by machinery. Highly skilled craftsmen and technicians may be able to keep their manual work to support their livelihoods, but everyone else is going to be pushed to unemployment or some sort of knowledge work. There are fewer and fewer knowledge jobs built around an hourly wage model, because in our faster and faster moving economy, value comes not from spending a certain amount of time punched in at an office, or logged in to a system, but by creating greater amounts of impact in lesser amounts of time. The growing trend of remote work is a sign of this ideal at work.

If a human arrives at an office every day, chatting around the coffee pot for thirty minutes before actually starting work, and then maybe walking around the office with a clipboard and a diligent countenance, their coworkers can generate a lot of assumptions about their work ethic, which are in fact totally separate from the quality or amount of the actual output. In many office settings, it isn't the person doing the best work that gets the most attention, it is the people who project diligence most effectively.

I am an advocate for at least a partial remote work schedule, because the person never seen at the office has no net to fall back on but her good work. The only evidence of her presence or participation is the work she produces, and the quality of that work is judged upon its own merit with very little subjective input, which is the best case scenario if your are good at what you do.

At this point you may detect agitation from your Ego, as you consider so straightforward an arrangement as being evaluated purely by your results. That's because the Ego has no interest in actually being held accountable to that standard—there is too much risk in being perceived as "less than." Being passed up for a promotion or a raise because of office politics is actually more tolerable for the Ego, because it can be rationalized away. Missing a promotion because you fell 10% short of a clear goal out in front of you leaves no room for the Ego to wiggle. To any uncertain outcome, the Ego assigns the same urgency as physical harm or even death. It's an entirely natural and human reaction because our Egos are always hard at work, maintaining the status quo in order to keep us safe. If we can see clearly why we think the way we do, we can better appreciate just how difficult it can be to change the pattern.

$1,000 For an Hour of Your Time

"One of the coolest and wisest hours a man has, is just after he awakes in the morning."
—Herman Melville, *Bartleby the Scrivener*

If you had to pay $1,000 an hour for your own time, what would be worth doing? Yes, for a 40-hour work week, 50 weeks a year, that's a $2,000,000 income. I can't promise you'll make that much immediately after reading this book, although I do believe in my bones that it is possible. I *can* promise you this: *Your time will never be more valuable than what you believe it is.*

If your time was suddenly worth $1,000/hour, what would you start doing, and more importantly, what would you stop doing? Even more telling: think of your time as *costing* you $1,000/hour to utilize. Now what would your days looks like?

Our culture is driven by consumption—food, cars, clothes, television, films, music, and books. We voraciously consume food and media, and we have lots of help in developing even better skills in that area, because of advertising. Unfortunately, there is no media machine pushing us to create and add value. The $1,000 question is: What is your daily balance of consumption versus creation? If you want to make truly amazing things happen in your life, focus on producing just a little more value than you consume, day in and day out. So many people are net consumers that just putting yourself on the net creator side by a small margin will set you far apart over time.

Once I started thinking about my balance of creation versus consumption each day, how I guarded my time started to change. I used to watch a LOT of movies at night, and play videogames frequently. Now, I track the balance of my day's activities, and only when I feel like I have spent enough hours in creation mode do I feel good about doing something consumeristic like playing video games—because I left my creation/consumption equation far in the positive.

Thinking this way also changed the way that I deployed my money. I spend a lot more on services now, and a lot less on stuff. I know that a word like "stuff" won't sound terribly articulate to the English majors out there, however, I choose that word intentionally, because buying stuff has been so glamorized in our society—I want to help bring things back into check. Most "stuff," like homes, cars, clothes, and toys, wear out over time, meaning we spend more and more of our precious time and energy dealing with depreciating assets. Most services, on the other hand, provide an experience that enhances over time, or frees us up to spend time elsewhere.

One of the single best purchases I have ever made was to hire a cleaning service for our house. This started when my wife Danielle enrolled in medical school. We foresaw our already limited free time together starting to dwindle. I thought I could be okay with a house that became slightly more of a mess on average, but Danielle knew that she would never be able to focus if she came home to a dirty hole. Hiring a cleaner means Danielle doesn't have to spend extra time away from studying, and it means that any magical free moments can be spent with friends, family, and each other, without the obligation of those chores pulling us away.

Because we assign such a high value to our time, the money we pay for that service is a screaming deal because of the time it frees up to use in more valuable ways. Perhaps you're not in a financial position to invest in something like a cleaner, but high income is not required to assign a $1,000 an hour value to your time. In fact, anyone who worked their way up to earning anything close to that actual hourly rate only did so because they valued their own time that highly first, and then slowly demonstrated that much value to other people, to the point that they were able to charge and earn that much.

Even if you're not in a position to hire a cleaner right now, even if you currently make minimum wage, you should still assign a high value to your time. Why? Because this transformation does not begin with something like hiring a cleaner—it begins with believing you should, and then acting accordingly. It's not the action that happens first, but the belief. Believing your time is valuable leads to a whole host of tiny decisions and behavior modifications that start adding up and compounding over time, leading inevitably to the financial freedom to hire services that lead to an enriching life.

One of those early shifts for me was my morning routine. I am very much a morning person. My best thinking happens early in the day. I used to start my day off with a diet of morning news, Facebook, and email. I came to realize that I was clouding my best thought-zone of the day by letting other people put random thoughts into my head. Now I give myself at least couple of hours in the morning to hear my own thoughts, when those thoughts are at their best. I save Facebook for the evening when most of my original thinking has gone to bed for the night anyway. Basic daylight management could be a huge breakthrough for you, too. There are a few creative geniuses who work best from 10pm to 3am (you know who you are), but I think most of us are in a natural rhythm that aligns more with the sun than the moon.

That's why I get up early every morning, usually at 5am. Choosing to get up early forces me to go to bed earlier, usually at 9pm. That one choice naturally shifts my awake time to a part of the day that I can use more productively. This would not work the same if I got up at 7am and went to bed at 11pm—I know because I had a post-college period of several months of unemployment during which I fell into a natural 7am awake to 11pm asleep rhythm. There is a natural period of the day, around 4–6pm, when other people are getting off work, when friends, family, and wives (well, just one) want to start interacting with me more, inviting me to dinner, or out to drinks. Those hours are no good for clear, solitary thinking. And for me, no matter what I try to shift, 7pm onward cannot be as productive as pre-11am. Like the age-old mother's adage, "nothing good happens after midnight," I realized I enjoy a baseline productivity in the morning that I just can't access at night. At this point in my life, when I have so much time out in front of me to plant seeds and watch them grow, I wanted to put the emphasis on the time that allows me to plant the most seeds.

This means for my first couple hours of every day, no news, no email, no social media. Just me and my thoughts. I do read, but only the books and articles that I have already chosen to add to my thinking. If there is something truly important in the news that morning, 10 people will be calling me, or I will see evidence of it out my windows. Otherwise, news or Facebook posts only give me someone else's ideas; ideas that will derail me from my best games, and place me into someone else's.

Quitting Toward Success

I constantly read and listen to messages from people who have produced the kinds of results I want to produce. I spend an hour almost every day studying success. That course of study led me to identify a lot of useless things I used to do, that I don't now. I used to set my alarm for the last possible moment I could get up, rush around to get ready, and still get to work on time. I thought I was maximizing my sleep. What I was really doing was maximizing my stress.

It is not so much the lack of capacity for greatness that holds us back, it is the lack of immunity from the things that pull us down.

If you are a person who doesn't like saying no, realize that saying yes to anything is also saying no to a lot of other things you could have been doing. If you focus on saying no to the opportunities that don't push you further down the path you have charted for yourself, all kinds of right opportunities will suddenly have room to materialize in front of you, inviting you to say yes to them. This will be *hard* and will mean saying no to many amazing opportunities. The way to stay strong is to remind yourself that you are reserving space for your most important pursuits. Remember the crucial question: If you had to pay $1,000 to occupy your own time, what would be worth doing? What would not be worth doing?

As you consider how to become more powerful in your productivity, the game moves you closer to activities you want to do, and adds barriers or friction between you and those you want to avoid. Social media can be immensely distracting, so I changed my password to something I wouldn't remember easily off the top of my head. Now I intentionally keep my browsers from automatically logging in, forcing me to go to my password manager every time I want to log in to Facebook. The barrier is not huge, but I had often found myself opening up a Facebook window in moments of downtime, without consciously choosing to do it. That password barrier forces me to make a conscious choice, and I can then reorient my time toward constructive reading rather than mindless browsing. This is not an anti-social media diatribe, I simply advocate for better curation of what we fit into our lives.

You may choose not to give up social media, and likewise there are activities that I will keep doing that you might choose to give up. I cook dinner almost every night because I love cooking and find it relaxing. You might find your life enriched by spending as little time in the kitchen as possible, to the point that hiring a chef would come before hiring cleaners. Only you can know what adds or subtracts value in your life.

I do know this: To get where you want to go, you *will* have to give up something you love doing now, to have something you will love more later. The quitting will be hard at first, it will be painful, and you will maybe even feel like you are not being true to yourself. You might have friends give you a hard time for the change, maybe even call you a sellout—that's why I recommend doing this quietly and not telling friends at first. The question to ask yourself is: *"Which version of myself do I want to be true to: the current me, or the higher version that I seek?"*

Just Beat Zero: How Propinquity Trumps Entropy

Propinquity describes the proximity or ease of access to something. I am a member of a specific gym only because it is literally a one-minute drive from my house. I knew I would be much less likely to go to the gym if it was hard to get to, so I picked the gym with the greatest propinquity. You can put propinquity into action with the following maxim: Getting started beats never doing anything.

Scouring the whole house for "spring cleaning" is a large undertaking, so thinking about the whole job at once can be daunting enough to make us delay the project indefinitely. Likewise, exercising in the early morning can be hard when bed is so cozy and warm, and the gym is on the other side of a cold, dark car ride. Excuses add up quickly, blocking us from our best intentions. Pursuing propinquity means reducing the friction between us and an activity, so we are more likely to just get up and take one step in the right direction. One step leads to two steps, then three, and before you know it, you're well on your way to success.

We can play games of propinquity to promote follow-through on our best intentions. Fitness clubs often recommend setting up your workout clothes and shoes in a neat pile before bed, making it mentally easier to jump up and go. The key in these moments is to shrink your commitment to the point that your mental burden becomes small enough to easily overcome, allowing you to launch into the activity. Maybe you say, "I just can't think about reading a whole chapter of a book right now." You could answer yourself with, "try reading one page, and then let's see how we feel." Or back to our gym example: If your brain will not agree to venture out into the cold, see if you can just do one set of push ups right there in your room. You probably won't get rock-hard abs or lose 20 pounds by replacing a full workout with one set of pushups, but you may be able to turn one set of pushups into the gateway drug to actually going to the gym.

Why is propinquity such a valuable tactic? Because it rivals entropy. Entropy is the tendency of any organization and order we create to break back down into disorder. What's worse, the second law of physics states that entropy will increase over time. Think about the last time you had a cleaning day and perfectly organized everything in your house—does that perfect order stay in place for long? Entropy is always at work; a natural force that is non-maliciously and persistently breaking down what we have built and returning it to a natural chaotic state. Productivity is important because entropy never takes a break. Any day that progress is zero, entropy wins. In order to make progress, we need to make sure that the few hours we have to produce value every day create more output than entropy breaks down.

So even if all you do is one set of pushups in your bedroom think about all the times that not exercising at all was the outcome. Now, think bigger than exercising: think about all the times in your life that you have wanted to do something, and doing nothing was the outcome. What would your life be like if every day was a day of progress, no matter how small? What if winning a day meant just beating zero, so that every day your progress compounded by at least a little bit? How small doesn't matter; more than zero is what matters.

CHAPTER 8

PUTTING THE "PERSONAL" BACK IN PERSONAL FINANCE

"Money isn't the most important thing in life, but it is reasonably close to oxygen."
—Zig Ziglar

Money Thoughts

I am a financial advisor, a money guy, so you might think I would have something to say about money. You are correct, but I bet you won't find the kind of advice here you expected. Nowhere will I pontificate on the right stock, bonds, or mutual funds to buy. I will not tell you how much to put into your IRA, ROTH, 401(K), 403(b), PSP, ESOP, ESPP, Coverdell, 529, SEP, or SIMPLE.

Many financial entertainers on television or radio programs spell out specific courses of action for their audiences to pursue. A call-in listener may even have the opportunity to give the host 10–30 seconds of background information and receive a detailed action plan for a major financial decision. These same celebrity sages publish books with specific "always" or "never" advice on savings, investment, retirement, insurances, real estate, or college funding.

My concern: At no stop along the way does the purchase of one of those books require verification of age, income, marital status, or current tax bracket. Much of the advice in those books may be wonderful plans of action *for a specific demographic*, yet it would be hard for an unchaperoned reader to know if any particular advice truly applies to him or his family.

The probable financial trajectory of a high school teacher is very different from that of a doctor in residency, never mind the huge difference in future guaranteed benefits a public employee receives, versus a doctor in private practice who has to save for herself. Even if the two of them made the same income right now, all the differences in future income and future benefits would create worlds of difference in the most effective paths for each of them to start saving for retirement. Even a book or website written specifically for the financial concerns of one profession, like doctors, would not be able to take into account all the differences in personal trajectory that each individual doctor experiences.

That is why my money thoughts here will be dedicated to building a philosophical framework around relating to money. If you like what you read, I am happy to have someone from my team introduce you to our work and see if our approach is a good fit for you. Just email us at learnmore@discoveryourpowers.com and we can help you schedule a phone call or find one of our upcoming webinars to learn more.

Identifying Your Money Thoughts

How do you relate to money in your life? For many of us, the answer to that question is heavily influenced by how our parents related to money when we were young. Maybe your parents didn't have a lot of money, so they helped you develop a set of outlooks and principles designed to deal with not having money, both positive and negative.

Some negative money thoughts, relating to scarcity:

Money isn't important; money doesn't buy happiness; I should get paid more for working this hard; those with a lot of money did something wrong to get it

Some positive money thoughts, relating to scarcity:

Waste not, want not; there is always enough; save, save, save; figure out a way to make do with what you have

Many amazing benefits can come from these kinds of thoughts. Very creative people tend to think this way, because creativity thrives in environments of scarcity. When there are giant heaps of money lying around, it is easy to throw cash at problems instead of seeking elegant solutions.

On the other side of the spectrum, there is the household with readily available cash, and all of the potential positive or negative thoughts that come with that:

Some negative money thoughts, relating to abundance:

I have so much to lose; I hope I don't mess this up

Some positive money thoughts, relating to abundance:

Money is a tool to serve the greater good; I don't need a lot to be happy; my income is a reflection of the value I produce

You may be surprised to learn that neither of these ways of thinking depends on the actual amount of cash we have on hand, but instead reflect the way our brains were trained to look at the world. Unfortunately, that training is often not that practical or helpful.

Money is one of the most emotional parts of our lives, and we are not typically trained in how to work with it, at least not in the same way we are trained for most other areas of our lives. Our parents work with us to learn how to ride a bike; our teachers force us to learn how to type, how to perform long division, and how to read. Where do we get the same level of attentive education on utilizing our money?

We receive very little formal training, so by default, we are taught by the media. Television and movies teach us there are very few consequences for our actions that can't be solved in an hour, and advertisers teach us to make financial decisions in the moment, based on momentary feelings and emotions. Every single advertisement we have ever seen boils down to: "Spend some money with us *right now*, and you will instantly feel better!"

What makes progress in this area truly challenging is that we usually *do* feel better if we take that advertiser's advice and buy the thing. The feeling just happens to be much more temporary than they would lead us to believe. I would like to arm you with a few tools to build an independent model for viewing money, and for making more powerful decisions where money is concerned.

The first step is to remove yourself from involuntary subscription to anyone else's money game. In my experience, most of us do things that support what we most want in life...*as long as we can stay present and focused on what it is we most want*. This is remarkably difficult to do, because marketers and advertisers have decades of experience distracting us from what we had already decided was most important, and focusing our attention on what they want us to buy.

Fictional 1960s advertising executive Don Draper was darn good at his job, and the real people of Madison Avenue have only grown more powerful over time. They have access to incredible amounts of research and data, and can harness more computing power in one project than all the early Madison Avenue creatives combined. Modern advertisers know exactly what to do and why, every single step of the way. When the colorful, sugary cereal is emblazoned with the most popular cartoon characters and placed on a shelf that perfectly corresponds with the eye level of a 4–8 year old, there is not a single accidental or unintentional decision in the whole process. We are not going to beat this industry at its own game.

Advertising is not going to go away, and becoming a total media hermit does not strike me as attainable for most, so what to do? Fighting harder against our culture's consumerism also feels like a losing battle, so I wouldn't suggest that, either. *Instead of fighting the good fight, why not change the rules?*

Here is what I know about myself: Telling me that I can't afford something is the best way to get me to buy it, and buy it quickly. I think I developed that instinct over the years since I first started my business, when I was making little money, and watching every single dollar come in and out of my checking account like each portrait of Washington or Hamilton was a clue to solving the DaVinci Code.

I was paid via autodeposit every Friday morning, and I had to make sure to fill my gas tank on the way to work every Friday, so I could travel to see clients over the following week. (I filled it on Friday, by the way, so I wouldn't accidentally spend that money over the weekend!) But, over time as my business grew, I developed a mental image of myself as a successful advisor, a provider, a giver of gifts, and someone who is generous with the abundance that has been given to me.

I also developed a twitch at any sign that I might be reverting back to my former state. This can generate ironic spending tendencies that would actually threaten to push me faster back toward my leaner life. Young me couldn't afford to fix the car I had, let alone buy a new one. Today, if I saw a car I couldn't afford but wanted, I might be tempted to focus on the financing options that would help me drive home in that beauty in the same day that I discovered it. Do you follow the irony? My emotions could lead me to buy a car, just to prove to myself that I have money. In order to prove to myself that I could buy a Rolls Royce (and hire a driver, because you don't buy a Rolls to sit in the front seat), I might stretch myself to a near financial breaking point. I don't bring this up as something unique to me. I think many of us use our money to prove something to ourselves or others, and doing so usually pushes us farther away from what we actually want. These are the powerful emotional contradictions that money creates in our lives.

I use cars as an example because many of us are trained to use vehicles as a measuring stick of our own or other's success. However, a car just means that someone found the necessary combination of cash flow and dealer incentives to drive off the lot with that vehicle. Furthermore, purchasing a vehicle only devours the cash flow required to invest in other important, longer-term assets. In other words, the people you see who look the nicest on the outside—cars, homes, clothes, toys—may actually have the most hollow financial insides.

In his book *Stop Acting Rich*, Thomas Stanley argues that most people we see driving the nicest cars usually don't have real financial wealth and stability. Have you ever known someone who had all the nicest cars they wanted in their youth and middle age, and now laments spending all their money because they have nothing but social security to live on and can barely afford their medication? Not ringing any bells? I wouldn't think so. We hear very few of these stories, because they are so painful and embarrassing to tell that the people living them don't even tell the real story to themselves. They blame the stock market, whoever the President was when they were starting their career, or some other situation that was out of their control.

The story of money in our lives is often difficult to get straight, because it is a story that plays out over such a long period of time. Because it is a cumulative story, our choices today are already writing the final chapter for us. By getting clear on the contradictions and misconceptions in your story about money right now, you can look ahead and preview the final chapter while there's still time for a rewrite.

A Saab Story

Several years ago, as I started gaining traction in my business, I was finally able to go out and buy a new car. The black Saab 9-3 was not brand new, but it was new to me, and in mint condition. The dealer felt it fit to mention that it was Microsoft co-founder Paul Allen's assistant that had traded in the car, inferring that this person's extensive travel schedule was the reason the car had such low mileage compared to the age. He was probably also trying to create some image of this car as a holy relic of the Seattle tech sector, thus deserving a premium price.

I was in trouble from the start, because from the moment the salesman pulled the car around for my test drive, I was in love. The deep silky black color, the leather interior, Scandinavia's special attention to cup holders, and the Turbocharger! When we sat down at the sales desk for the negotiation phase, I *knew* I was going to walk out of there with the keys. (Small life lesson: If at the start of any negotiation you are *committed* to walking out with the item in question, know that you have also committed to spending the maximum amount possible to get what you want.) I was generating enough cashflow to pay for the car, yet looking back I realize I paid a greater proportion of my monthly income toward that car payment than I would now recommend for any client in the same position.

The car salesman was about my age, and at least as new or newer in his career than I was in mine. This goes to show that when we play someone else's game, we will almost always lose. Even if we play our own game at a higher level than they play theirs, when we enter their arena, they are still the expert. This is why so many professional athletes are targeted by dishonest advisors coming after them to invest money in "unique opportunities." The higher the athlete is at his game, the more likely he is to feel like he can win at anything, making it yet more likely that he will lose at someone else's game.

The turning point of the car negotiation was my answer to a critical question: "What can you afford?" I threw out what I thought was a reasonable monthly payment (remember, I *wanted* that car). He then asked: "If we can get you that monthly payment, are you walking out of here with that car today?" I was amazed that this was going so well! What I didn't realize was the monthly payment was not even close to the most important number. Total price for a car is the first number to lock in, because the same monthly payment inserted into different interest and amortization schedules can produce a vastly different total cost for a car over time. I am not particularly fast on my feet with numbers, especially if I am thinking about any other factors at the same time. (You might be surprised at that fact in a financial advisor, although I think it makes me better and more dependable—you know I am not making anything up as I go along!)

The result of all this is that a couple of years later, reviewing the amortization schedule paperwork, I realized I did not receive quite as good a deal as I thought, because what I thought was a four-year payment schedule had actually been switched to a five-year schedule somewhere along the way. I don't begrudge the salesman; it actually wasn't his job to get me the best deal, it was his job to sell me the car. We all know that the car industry is set up that way, and he never declared otherwise. The whole problem is that I tacitly agreed to play his game, instead of declaring my own.

When he started by asking what I could afford, that was my opportunity to change the whole game. Instead of answering that question, I could have countered with a powerful statement: "It is not about what I can afford, it is only a matter of whether we can fit this into the game I have created." If I said something like that, then his very next words would have to be something like: "What is your game?" or, "What are you talking about?", or "Are you crazy?" As a good salesman wanting to understand the customer, he would have no choice but to ask that clarifying question. That gives me the opportunity to redefine the whole conversation and place both of us in *my* game. I could have said something like:

"Well, I have built a set of strategies to tell my money where to go, instead of wondering later where it went. I want to create and maintain financial balance in my life, and I have a lot of other big goals that are important to me. With that in mind, I have dedicated X% of my monthly income to a car purchase. I would really enjoy fitting this car into that strategy, and at the same time I need to be clear: Because I am playing a game built around realizing some amazing long-term goals, sticking to the strategy is much more important to me than getting this car."

That last part of the speech would actually have been for my benefit, not the salesman's. You remember my twitch whenever the question "Can I afford it?" comes up? With that last sentence I would have inoculated myself from the twitch. I know I will need a reminder of the game I am playing and why I am committed to it. Based on the same principles as our Affirmation Statements from way back in Chapter One, the best way to stay present to my strategy is to say it out loud. Now the whole situation is not about affording or not affording anything, it becomes about fulfilling a strategy I have carefully crafted to bring me closer to the full version of the life I want to live. It is about *having a thing I want that is even bigger than a car*.

Of course I didn't have that perspective back then, and I walked out of there paying more for the car than I could have, and more than was really constructive for my life at that point. Your very own financial mistake may come to mind at this point, and if it is more recent than mine, the wound may still be raw. I encourage you to allow yourself grace and forgiveness for what happened. Hanging on to guilt for past mistakes is the surest way to repeat them. Instead, acknowledge what happened, release it, and go about building a stronger financial platform for the future.

Personal Financial Statement

The first step in building resistance to the financial games of others is to write out your personal financial statement (PFS). This is a paragraph that outlines the primary motivations you seek to support when making financial decisions. Here is the actual PFS I have on my iPhone, which I read almost every morning along with my Affirmation Statements (the "we" here refers to me and my wife, Danielle):

We occupy our time with activities that create value for ourselves and our community. When we create currency, a portion of that value is always given away in generosity, and a portion is always planted to grow and create more value, before any portion is set aside for consumption. When we consume currency, our primary goals are to reduce stress in our lives, and make others' lives better.

I believe that continually practicing gratitude helps decrease stress and produces a better, more fulfilling life, and I think one of the most effective ways to maintain an attitude of thankfulness is to act generously. How can you not be grateful for everything you have, when you're in the middle of a generous act? I think it's pretty hard.

I also believe that given the chance, the "urgent now" will always crowd out the "important future," and this is a temptation we should try our best to resist. Saving for the winter of our lives is part of an important future, while buying the newest iPhone and the latest Washington microbrew is an urgent now. I choose to contribute to the future me first, or the present me will likely spend all the money before I get to the future. When Danielle and I spend money, I remind myself of the types of purchases that end up producing real fulfillment and happiness. Filling up my house with more possessions has a rapidly diminishing, marginal return. Spending money on services that give us more time for the life we love is a huge win, and making others smile is even better.

Money Can't Buy Power

If we take a step back and look at money objectively, we can see that money is actually a neutral resource. The cultural idea that money is evil comes from the persistently misquoted biblical passage about money as the "root of all evil." The actual passage states that the "*love* of money is the root of all kinds of evil" (1 Timothy 6:10, KJV, my emphasis). Money can beat cancer, or fund a terrorist cell—it only magnifies the positive or negative energy we put into the world.

When negative energy rises, we might use our money to buy the shoes, gadgets, or meals that we can't afford or would not be healthy for us, as a way of self-soothing. When positive energy is in full force, we are more likely to use our money to help others, or pursue experiences that produce even more happiness. If you are already a jerk, add some money and you will be a rich jerk. If you are a saint, add a bunch of money and you will be a saint who marshals her resources to make an incredible difference in many lives.

Money and power are closely intertwined. Money is not needed to have power, and growing power does tend to lead to growing your money. Both money and power are neutral resources that share a common relative: Value. Power is the ability to create increased value in the world, for yourself and others; and money just happens to be the most prevalent way that our world uses to track, exchange, and store value. Money is the least important of the three, because no matter what happens, the cultivation of power and the creation of value for others will always enable you to create more money. Money is merely a cosmic Fitbit to help you track your steps across a landscape of choices.

Lest I leave you with any kind of "more is better" message, I will say that having more money is not the end all be all. Throughout my life, I have had less money and I've had more money, and I definitely prefer more—it's just that "more and less" are something we all get to define. I have seen lots of examples of people with relatively more, or relatively less, money, and I can unequivocally state that having more or less money had less to do with happiness than how the families had designed their lives. Pursuing more for the sake of more only leads to discontent and despair. Whether we are talking about money or power, design the dream for your ideal life first, and use that as a guide for how much more of anything you need to pursue it, because fulfillment probably requires less than you think.

CHAPTER 9

BECOMING THE HERO IN YOUR OWN LIFE

Remember that annoyingly successful person from the back cover of the book? How do you know that you are not already that person to someone else? There will always be someone who is bigger, faster, better, richer, or smarter than you, and you knew that before reading this book. If there will always be someone better than you at everything, then stop and acknowledge your place in the cycle: accept that someone else is looking at you right now, as the better version of themselves. If you can see that, then you can see that the game is really about perspective. No one is really above anyone else in any truly meaningful way, and no one can be who you want to be better than you.

In a book that will probably be classified as "self-improvement," I can't let you leave without making it clear that you do not need to be fixed. You are a whole and complete being, as-is, right now. Any dissatisfaction you may have about yourself or your life is just grit in the gears. The machinery is just fine; the foreign material that worked itself into the mix is the only thing I want to help clean out. To come at you with a different metaphor, have you ever made a copy of a copy? Each time another copy is copied, taking a step farther from the original, the image becomes more grainy and starts to fade away. All I suggest is that you may be seeing a copy of a copy of your true self, and clearing away those copies to be the fullest version of yourself means people will marvel at the clarity and living color of who you really are.

Whether or not you are currently happy with the version of yourself you are today, can you own the value of who you are? No one can replicate the whole of you, so if you lean in to your "you-ness," you will have exactly zero competition, because you will be the sole player in a market only you can create.

Fair warning: Your Ego is going to fight you tooth and nail along the way. The best way to win is not to fight back. Starting a fight just gives the Ego more energy to run. The first time you try something from this book that you thought was really cool and really scary, you Ego is going to jump out and try to stop you. Just say "thanks buddy, I appreciate the protection you have provided me all these years, and I just don't need it anymore."

So Now What?

You have two choices: You could be entertained, or you could be empowered. Being entertained means you have some warm fuzzy feelings in your tummy; you feel *good* after reading this book. You smile, set it down, and go back to doing everything you were doing before. You might carry some energy about it into the next few days, but you really aren't going to do anything. Being empowered means you will make a choice that something will be different. Being empowered means you may not exactly feel *good* right now—like the butterflies right before a performance, you may be nervous about what you now know you want or need to do to move yourself closer to the life you dream of. You might be on the precipice of upending the major arrangements of your life. You might already be practicing most of what I suggested here, but one big thing sticks out in your mind that you've been putting off.

Whether it is a metamorphosis or a minor tweak, you will most likely default to being entertained unless you take a tangible, actionable step within the next 24 hours. I am not kidding around here—if you have never been a doer, if you have a pattern of thinking without acting, then the rest of your life is at stake in the next 24 hours. I know the timing is not convenient, and it just so happens that the stars aligned for you to read this book right now, at this exact moment. Instead of thinking about reasons why not, why not just choose right now as the time to take action on that thing which has been almost happening in your life for however long. Interrupt that pattern *now*, or you could wake up in 20 years wondering what happened.

By now I hope you realize that power is not so much a resource to be collected, as it is a pattern of choices and actions. In this moment, you have a very simple choice between who you are now, and the vision of who you could become—that person you can see now, just on the edge of the horizon.

ABOUT THE AUTHOR

Author and financial advisor Cory Shepherd has 16+ years of experience in leading and coaching others toward living life more fully. Cory has gained national recognition as a leader in the financial industry. From building a team of over 30 advisors before age 30, to speaking and writing for national organizations, to coaching and counseling clients across the country, Cory's focus remains on helping others live powerfully and abundantly.

Cory is based in Seattle and is home wherever he and his wife Danielle happen to be.